MW00529030

GROWTH

⑦ ⑥ ③ ⑤ ④

GOODNESS · TRUTH · PERFECTION · CLARITY · JUSTICE · SELF CONTROL

**1**

HELPFULNESS · ALTRUISM · LOVING · BOLD · SERVANTS HEART · DISCERNING NEEDS

**2**

EFFICIENCY · ACTION · ENCOURAGER · ESTABLISHER · INSPIRING · EXCELLENCE

**3**

CREATIVITY · EMPATHY · LOVE OF BEAUTY · SPACE SAVER · EMOTIONALLY HONEST

**4**

WISDOM · VISION · STEADFASTNESS · CLARITY · FAITHFULNESS · HUMILITY

**5**

COURAGE · GUARDIANSHIP · KINDNESS · LOYALTY · STRENGTH · FAITHFULNESS

**6**

SPONTANEITY · JOY · THANKFULNESS · HOPE · LONG SUFFERING · VISION

**7**

STRENGTH · ZEAL · VIGILANT · JUSTICE · PROTECTOR · TENDERNESS

**8**

PEACE · KINDNESS · EMPATHY · PATIENCE · GENTLENESS · UNDERSTANDING

**9**

# WHAT PEOPLE ARE SAYING ABOUT ELISABETH BENNETT AND
## *THE ACHIEVER: GROWING AS AN ENNEAGRAM 3*

Elisabeth's biblical knowledge and extensive coaching experience pay off in this must-read book for Achievers. Using a laser-focused approach on my core strengths and weaknesses, I felt myself growing daily into the person God created me to be. Pick up this book and let yourself be encouraged and challenged so that you can find God's definition of success.

—*Tyler Zach*
Author, *The Gospel for Enneagram* series

As an Enneagram Three who values drive, ambition, and action, I often struggle to find where my story fits in Scripture. Elisabeth has done an incredible job distilling the truths of the Bible into relevant and practical devotions for this Achiever! If you're looking for a resource to help you fully live out God's creation for you, read this practical and actionable devotional.

—*Brian Dixon*
Co-founder, hope*writers
Business coach, BrianDixon.com

Elisabeth has written a delightful devotional full of important information for those who want to grow in their own self-awareness and relationship with Christ. I highly recommend reading this book so you can experience transformation on a much deeper level that will bring about the change you desire in life.

—*Beth McCord*
YourEnneagramCoach.com
Author of 10 Enneagram books

As with any typing system, it's easy to become enamored with profiling yourself and others to see where we *fit* in the world. What's harder is transferring the wisdom into practical applications toward actual growth, which is what Elisabeth Bennett does so well. These short, accessible devotional readings are a tool to help you connect with Scripture and not only grow in personal wholeness, but also relational awareness and connection with God. This is not a book about your Enneagram type with God sprinkled in; this is an invitation to be formed by Christ using the wisdom of your Enneagram type to help ask the right questions.

—*Adriel Booker*
Author, *Grace Like Scarlett*
Host, Tethered

Elisabeth has a beautiful way of guiding the reader into a deeper understanding and self-awareness that leads to spiritual growth through the Enneagram. Through biblically sound and practical devotions, she helps you move from, "Okay, I know what type I am but what's next?" to personal, relational, and spiritual growth, so that you can live in the fullness of who you were created to be in your unique type.

—*Justin Boggs*
The Other Half Podcast
Enneagram coach, speaker, entrepreneur

Through her beautifully articulate words, Elisabeth accurately portrays the shadow side of each Enneagram type while also highlighting the rich grace and freedom found in the spiritual journey of integration. Pairing Scripture with reflection questions and prayers, the devotions help guide the reader on the pathway of personal and spiritual growth in a powerful way that is unique to their type.

—*Meredith Boggs*
The Other Half Podcast

If you know your Enneagram type and you're ready to make meaningful steps toward growth, this book is for you. Elisabeth combines her Enneagram expertise with her deep faith to guide readers toward self-understanding, growth, and transformation through contemplative yet practical writing. This devotional is a great tool that you'll return to again and again.

—*Steph Barron Hall*
Nine Types Co.

# 60-DAY
# ENNEAGRAM DEVOTIONAL

## the
# ACHIEVER

## GROWING AS AN ENNEAGRAM

# ELISABETH BENNETT

WHITAKER
HOUSE

Introduction images created by Katherine Waddell.
Photo of Elisabeth Bennett by Jena Stagner of One Beautiful Life Photography.

## THE ACHIEVER
**Growing as an Enneagram 3**

www.elisabethbennettenneagram.com
Instagram: @enneagram.life
Facebook.com/enneagramlife

ISBN: 978-1-64123-570-9
eBook ISBN: 978-1-64123-571-6
Printed in the United States of America
© 2021 by Elisabeth Bennett

Whitaker House
1030 Hunt Valley Circle
New Kensington, PA 15068
www.whitakerhouse.com

Library of Congress Cataloging-in-Publication Data (Pending)

1 2 3 4 5 6 7 8 9 10 11 **UJ** 28 27 26 25 24 23 22 21

# DEDICATION

*To every Three holding this book,*
*your worth is immeasurable and permanent in Christ.*

# Contents

# FOREWORD

I remember that day in third grade as vividly as just about any other. It was my first day in a new school in a new state. As a shy kid who preferred to express himself through sports, I was terrified to leave the suburban life I knew for a small rural town hundreds of miles away. On that first day, I quietly took my cues from others to get by. Then it was time for math, and the teacher announced that we'd play a game of "around the world" to work on our multiplication. The game was simple. You stood next to a classmate's desk, the teacher held up a flashcard with a math problem, and the first one to blurt out the correct answer got to move on to the next desk. You kept standing as long as you kept winning.

My turn to be *it* came. I gulped, took a deep breath, and readied myself. I was a good student, but so much attention so soon felt like a blinding spotlight. The first problem came, and I won. Then I won again. And again. And again. I lapped the classroom a few times before the teacher suggested we give someone else a turn. My suburban school was a month or two ahead of this country school in multiplication and I used it to my advantage. I had to work to sit down because I felt like I could fly. I felt like I could do anything.

My achievement gave me a sense of worth and accomplishment that day, and it felt incredible. So much of a type Three's life is formed, marked, and motivated by similar events. Granted, winning a multiplication game because I had a head start is no real achievement. But to a young type Three, it was fuel for the message I desperately wanted to believe: *I'm NOT a nobody. I'm a somebody.*

It took me well into my adulthood to realize what a fool's errand this type of thinking is. To be honest, it's a lesson I have to learn every day of my life. Such is the plight of a Three: a perpetual pursuit of manufacturing value and worth through achievement. When we Threes take some time to slow down and truly be honest with ourselves—not something we particularly enjoy—we come face to face with what's really behind it all. We're good at getting things done and looking good while doing it because we're afraid that if we stop, there may not be anything valuable or worthy about us.

This is the tragic irony of Threes: we're good at many things because we're afraid we're not good enough to *just be ourselves*. This false belief can lead us to all sorts of difficult and unsavory places. Left unchecked, we can fake it very well through life... until we fake ourselves.

If we're willing, God offers us hope that frees us from the unrelenting striving and ambition. It's not an easy lesson to learn because it doesn't require our typical tricks and strategies. If we slow down enough to truly listen, we can hear a God who speaks to our value and worth for who we are as beloved ones in Christ, which transcends the accomplishments we rack up.

I'm thankful for voices like Elisabeth's, those who understand the Three's plight and are patient enough to instill in these messages the things we need to hear. I'm also thankful for sixty days of reinforcement of that message. For my fellow type Threes reading this, a word of encouragement: the journey to live as a human *being*, not just a human *doing*, requires a different sort of work than we're used to. Our energetic productivity won't get us there. Flying through these sixty days in record time won't help. In fact, it will work against us. For those reading this to better understand the Threes in their lives, be more patient with us than we are with ourselves.

Elisabeth's devotions help us Threes lovingly surrender the things that tend to hinder us for that which is infinitely better. Our worth is not found in the things we do, but in a God who deems us worthy for simply being who our Creator created us to be. From this authentic place, our gifts of achievement can be used for all sorts of good and beautiful things.

Savor these pages in every sense of the word. Take your time. Digest. Revisit. Ponder. Reflect. Learn what it means to *be* with them.

—Drew Moser, Ph.D.
Author, *The Enneagram of Discernment:
The Way of Vocation, Wisdom, and Practice*
Co-host, Fathoms | An Enneagram Podcast

# ACKNOWLEDGMENTS

My journey from young hopeful writer, all the way back to the tender age of four, to holding books with my name on them hasn't been easy or pretty. In fact, it's held a lot of hurt, disappointment, and rejection. However, as you hold a book with my name on the cover in your hands, I'd love you to know who and what has sustained me through it all. You are holding a piece of God's redemption in my story, tangible proof of His kindness, and testament of His faithfulness. I didn't break any doors down or *do* anything myself that ensured my trajectory of publishing. God in His kindness handed me this opportunity, and to Him alone belongs all the glory and praise.

My agent Amanda deserves the highest of thanks and admiration. Thank you for answering my many questions, guiding, and giving me the confidence to do this. I couldn't have done it without you. To all the people at Whitaker House, my editor Peg and publisher Christine, thank you for making these devotionals what they are today. It's been a pleasure working with you all.

To my writing community hope*writers, thank you for giving me the courage to call myself a writer long before I felt like one. To Drew Moser of @Enneagrammers, thank you for being one of the first people to lay eyes on this devotional and for contributing so much wisdom to the Enneagram. I'm so grateful you wrote the foreword for this devotional, and for your heart for your fellow Threes.

Thank you to Pastor Bubba Jennings at Resurrection Church for reading over my proposal and giving me advice on how to serve Jesus well in this process.

The people who have been the biggest support and help to me during this process, and if I'm honest, my life, are:

Jena Stagner, thank you for being a consistent and loyal source of wisdom and encouragement in my life. Your energy is infectious, your humility is beautiful, and your drive to learn more about God is one of my favorite things. I am so grateful Threes will get to learn from you via this devotional. Thank you for sharing.

My mom, Diane, the only reason we didn't turn out to be those weird homeschool kids is because of your social awareness, extroversion, and drive. You have taught me so much about how to be a good friend, how to be generous, and how to get things done. You're by far my favorite Three.

Camille Jett, thank you for being our resident Three on the 3ish_andiknowit page. I'm so grateful for your dedication and drive to use your gifts for God's glory.

To all of the other Threes in my life who have left a big impact on my heart, as well as my ability to write this devotional, all my Enneagram Three clients, and a couple other suspected Threes whom I won't publicly *type* here, thank you!

John and Jan Bennett, thank you for faithfully praying for me and supporting me through this entire process. Your encouragement has moved mountains and sustained me on the hardest days.

Thank you, Mom and Dad (Joe and Diane Upton), for literally teaching me to read and write and encouraging me to say yes to big things. I would never have had the foundation to say yes without you and how you raised me. I'm so proud and grateful to have the two of you in my corner cheering me on.

Peter, you've been beyond supporting, patient, and caring toward me. I don't know what else I would've expected from a One. You have taught me so much about what it means to be faithful, and you never let me quit. You believe in me enough for both of us, and I can't believe the gift that you are in my life. You're my best friend and I love you.

# INTRODUCTION
## What Is the Enneagram?

The Enneagram is an ancient personality typology for which no one really knows the origins.

It uses nine points within a circle—the word itself means "a drawing of nine"—to represent nine distinct personality types. The points are numbered simply to differentiate between them, with each point having no greater or less value than the others. The theory is that a person assumes one of these personalities in childhood as a reaction to discovering the world as a scary, unkind place and thus unlikely to accept his or her true self.

The nine types are identified by their numbers or by these names:

1. The Perfectionist
2. The Helper
3. The Achiever
4. The Individualist
5. The Thinker
6. The Guardian
7. The Enthusiast
8. The Challenger
9. The Peacemaker

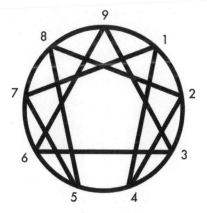

## HOW DO I FIND MY TYPE?

Your Enneagram type is determined by your main motivation. Finding your Enneagram type is a journey, as we are typically unaware of our motivations and instead focus on our behaviors. Many online tests focus on behaviors, and while some motivations *may* produce certain behaviors, this may not always be the case and you are unlikely to get accurate results.

To find your Enneagram type, you need to start by learning about *all* nine Enneagram types, and exploring their motivations in contrast to your own behaviors and deeper motivations.

You can ask for feedback from those around you, but most often, the more you learn, the clearer your core number shines through.

It's often the number whose description makes you feel the most *exposed* that is your true core type. Your core Enneagram number won't change, since it's solidified in childhood.

Each number's distinct motivation:

1. Integrity – Goodness
2. Love – Relationships
3. Worth – Self-Importance
4. Authenticity – Unique Identity
5. Competency – Objective Truth
6. Security – Guidance
7. Satisfaction – Freedom
8. Independence – Control
9. Peace – Equilibrium

## IS THIS JOURNEY WORTH IT?

Yes! The self-awareness you gain along the way is gold, and learning about the other types in the process brings you so much empathy and understanding for all of the other personalities in your life.

## WHAT MAKES THE ENNEAGRAM UNIQUE AND DIFFERENT FROM MYERS-BRIGGS, STRENGTHSFINDER, OR DISC ASSESSMENTS?

The Enneagram, unlike other typology systems, is fluid. Yes, the Enneagram tells you what your base personality characteristics are, but it also reveals how you change when you're growing, stressed, secure, unhealthy, healthy, etc.

You are not the same person at twenty as you are at sixty. You're not the same person at your stressful workplace as you are when binge-watching your favorite TV show and eating ice cream at home. The Enneagram accounts for these inconsistencies and changes in your behavior and informs you of when or how those changes occur.

If you look at the following graph, you'll see that each of the numbers connects to two other numbers by arrows. The arrow pointed toward your number is your growth arrow; the arrow pointed away is your stress number. When your life leaves you with more room to breathe, you exhibit positive characteristics of your growth number, and when you're stretched thin in seasons of stress, you exhibit the negative characteristics of your stress number.

This is one explanation for big shifts in personality over a lifetime.

Another point of difference between the Enneagram and other typology systems is *wings*. Your wings are the two numbers on either side of your core number, which add flavor to your per-

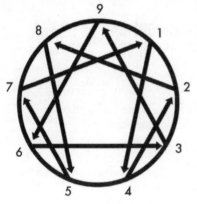

sonality type. Although your core number won't change—and your main motivation, sin proclivities, and personality will come from that core number—your wings can be very influential on your overall personality and how it presents itself. There are many different theories about wings, but the viewpoint we hold to is:

+ Your wing can only be one of the two numbers on either side of your core number. Therefore, you can be a 3 with a 4 wing (3w4) but not a 3 with a 5 wing (3w5).

+ You have access to the numbers on either side of your number, but most people will only have one dominant wing. (*Dominant* meaning you exhibit more of the behaviors of one wing than the other wing.) It is possible to have equal wings or no wing at all, but this is rare.

+ Your dominant wing number can change from one to the other throughout your life, but it's speculated this might only happen once.

As you read through this book, we will go over what an Enneagram Three looks like with both of its wings. If you're struggling to figure out what your core number is, this book series could really help give you some more in-depth options!

## HOW DO YOU BECOME YOUR TYPE?

Personality is a kind of shield we pick up and hide behind. It is functional, even protective at times, but altogether unnecessary because God made us in His image from the start. However, we cling to this personality like it's our key to survival, and nothing has proven us wrong so far. It's the only tool we've ever had, and the shield has scratches and dents to prove its worth.

Not all parts of our personality are wrong or bad, but by living in a fallen, sinful world, we all tend to distort even good things in bad ways. Amen?

What personality did you pick up in childhood? If you're reading this devotional, then you may have chosen type Three. Your need to have worth became the one thing that your life would rotate around from early childhood until right now, at this very moment.

The Enneagram talks about childhood wounds and how we pick a particular shield as a reaction to these wounds. However, not all siblings have the same Enneagram type even though they heard the same wounding message or had the same experiences growing up. This is because we are born with our own unique outlook on the world, and we filter everything through that outlook. You and your siblings may have heard the same things, but while you heard, "You're only loved when you're successful," your sister heard, "You're only loved when you're helping." Thus, you both would become different Enneagram types.

Trauma and abuse of all kinds can definitely impact your choice of shield as well. If you think of all these nine shields as being a different color, perhaps you were born predisposed to be more likely to pick blue than red. However, in a moment of early trauma, you might have heard someone shouting, "Pick black! Black is the only option!" Thus, you chose black instead of blue, which would've been your own unique reaction to your life circumstances. It's hard to say how these things happen exactly, especially when trauma is involved. Are you who you are *despite* trauma…or because of it? Only God knows, but there is healing and growth to be found either way.

We've all heard the phrase, "You can't teach an old dog new tricks." I'd like to propose that when referencing personality, it might be said, "The longer you use your personality, the harder it is to see its ineffectiveness." It's not impossible for an older person to drastically change for the better, but it will be harder for them to put down what has worked for them for so long. That's why, as we age, it can become harder to even see where our personality ends and our true self begins. Even if the unhealthy parts of our personality have been ineffective, they still seem to be the only things that have worked for us.

## WHY DO WE NEED THE ENNEAGRAM WHEN WE HAVE THE HOLY SPIRIT AND THE BIBLE TO GUIDE US?

The Enneagram is a helpful tool, but only when it is used as such. The Enneagram cannot save you—only Jesus can do that.

However, God made us all unique, and we all reflect Him in individual ways. Learning about these unique reflections can encourage us, as well as point us toward our purposes. The Enneagram also reveals the sin problems and blind spots of each type with which you may unknowingly struggle. Revealing these can lead us to repentance and change before God.

## HOW DO I CHANGE MY MORE NEGATIVE BEHAVIORS?

Alcoholics Anonymous was really on to something when they called their first step "admitting you have a problem." How do you solve a problem if you don't know you have one or are in denial about it? You can't. If you have a shield you're using to protect yourself from the world, but are blissfully unaware of its existence, you won't understand how its very existence impacts you and your relationships. You definitely won't be putting that battered but battle-tested shield of a personality down anytime soon.

Similar to the wisdom of admitting one has a problem before recovery can begin, the Enneagram proposes self-knowledge as the starting point before there can be change.

Whether you're 100 percent sure you are an Enneagram Three, or just curious about the possibility, this is what it looks like to be a Three.

# WHAT IT MEANS TO BE AN ACHIEVER

The Enneagram Three is considered the Achiever. They have a lot of energy, are highly socially aware, and tend to thrive when they're getting things done. Achievers are motivated by worth, especially self-worth, which they are busy building up by adding worth and value to the world around them.

These traits often shine the brightest in Threes' teen years, when they are coming into their own and when they're pretty adept at reading what is needed of them to succeed. They're also painfully aware of how they look to others, which can cause a great deal of stress and anxiety.

Tyler can remember dreaming about getting a particular car when he turned sixteen; it was sporty and would make him look really cool. But when his parents took him car shopping, they didn't take his preferences into consideration and bought a car that was ugly—just to save a little extra money. He was unbelievably disappointed that they ignored his wishes and gave him a car that he felt ashamed to drive. He knew that their reasons might've been logical, but it didn't change his humiliation every time he pulled up to school in his not-so-dream-worthy first car.

Nevertheless, Tyler was busy building up his worth in other ways during high school as he had always been an entertainer, a go-getter, and thrived off being seen as a leader. Tyler was pictured again and again in his local town newspaper for different leadership and athletic accolades during his teen years, and this is still something he reflects on with pride. He was a role model to many as the wrestling captain, student council president, and homecoming king. In college, he was president of his fraternity.

Tyler is an Enneagram Three, and the Enneagram has helped him appreciate his unique gifts of optimism, drive, and giving encouragement. He didn't realize how powerful those gifts were until he learned about the Enneagram and saw those gifts named in himself by his type.

It can be argued that no one gets as much done as a type Three; that is why they're so accurately called the Achiever. Whether they're completing the task at hand, climbing the corporate ladder, or turning on the charm, Threes should not be underestimated.

Threes are one of the least understood numbers on the Enneagram. They tend to project what they believe others want to see, and this can make them difficult for others to decipher. Words like *deceit*, *chameleon*, and *performer* are often assigned to the Three. Yet I often hear Threes reject these words, as they know they have good intentions toward people and want everyone to feel comfortable around them.

Threes all have a vision of what success looks like that is as unique as each individual Three. Some Threes want to be an Olympic tennis star, some aspire to head a corporation, while others fixate on relational success. It all depends on what they value and what they think will bring them the most worth in their specific social circles.

Healthy Threes are very likable people; they're charming without being fake, genuinely interested in others, and have energy for days. On the other hand, unhealthy Threes will be horribly unaware of themselves, changing their personality to fit what they think others want them to be, taking whatever attention they can get, and never admitting their mistakes

# ALL ABOUT BEING A THREE

## MOTIVATION

**Worth**—to be admired and praised for their achievements. To add genuine value to the world, to be distinguished from others.

Threes want to prove to themselves and others that they add value to the world. This unquenchable thirst for value/worth often leads Threes to shed their quirks, becoming more approachable to others in order to become successful. Each Three's gauge of what success is will be different, but each Three exhibits the drive to achieve whatever they view as success.

## BIGGEST FEAR

*Being worthless, a failure, or others finding their efforts lacking.*

## HEART TRIAD

Each Enneagram type is dominant in either feeling, thinking, or doing. We refer to these *triads* as heart-centered, head-centered, and gut-centered.

Threes, along with Twos and Fours, are considered to be part of the heart triad. This means they first process information as feelings before moving on to thinking or doing. In the most practical sense, this means that actions from others tend to feel very personal, as information is first processed as feeling before it can be thought through logically. Those in the heart triad may be told they are too sensitive when they react out of "how does this make me feel?"

Each of the three triads has a defining emotion connected to the center that is a stumbling block for them. For the heart triad, this emotion is shame. Twos, Threes, and Fours struggle to believe that they have inherent worth and believe they must do something in order to have worth.

As we know from Scripture, God formed us in the womb of our mother, and it is He who gives us worth. This means that our worth cannot be taken away from us, we cannot earn our worth, and we cannot add more worth to ourselves by *doing* anything.

Matthew 6:26 says, *"Look at the birds of the air: they neither sow nor reap nor gather into barns, and yet your heavenly Father feeds them. Are you not of more value than they?"*

This is a rhetorical question, to which the answer is, "Yes, of course, we are worth more than birds." But why? Because God made us in His own image, with thoughts, feelings, desires, and dominion here on earth.

> *So God created man in his own image, in the image of God he created him; male and female he created them. And God blessed them. And God said to them, "Be fruitful and multiply and fill the earth and subdue it, and have dominion over the fish of the sea and over the birds of the heavens and over every living thing that moves on the earth."*
>
> (Genesis 1:27–28)

God is the One who gave us our worth. The God who put the breath in your lungs gave you value that you can't lose. How much time do we waste doubting that value? For those of us in the heart triad, the answer is likely a lot!

Shame comes into play when Satan uses the lie "You'll never be worth anything" to paralyze Threes and condemn them. If he cannot destroy you and your future, Satan will try to steal your peace and the good works God has set before you to do.

## CHILDHOOD WOUND

The wounding childhood message Threes heard (or thought they heard) was, "It is not okay to have your own identity and feelings," or "Your emotions and true self aren't wanted here." Threes grew up thinking their worth and identity was found in their achievements, and that any identity not founded in success was worthless. Feelings felt messy—as if they were in the way—so young Threes learned to process them quickly and shove unwanted emotions away.

This could've been because success was a high priority in their family, they were told that feelings were selfish or wrong, or they grew up in a chaotic environment and thus clung to success and working hard as the keys to achieving stability.

## THE LOST CHILDHOOD MESSAGE THREES LONG TO HEAR

### "You Are Loved for Who You Are"

The lost message Threes long to hear is, "You are loved for who you are." If you fail, if you lose everything, if you can't do whatever you're trying to do, if you need a break—God's love for you won't change. His love does not depend on your success or achievements. He literally cannot love you any more than He does at this moment. Let yourself rest in Him.

## DEFENSE MECHANISM

### *Identification*

Identification or chameleoning is the defense mechanism Threes use to be liked and accepted by others. Threes are very socially aware and can often hear what others want from them loud and clear. Sometimes it doesn't even occur to a Three to not give the person what they want. This is identification. *Does this person want me to be a conservative Christian or more progressive? Do they hate country music? Well, then I won't mention that I love it.* Threes do this so effortlessly in their life that it often feels like the way to love others or to best behave, when in reality they are suppressing parts of themselves in order to be accepted by others.

## WINGS

A wing is one of the numbers on either side of your Enneagram number that adds some *flavor* to your type. You'll still be your core number in essence, but your wing can impact a lot of your behaviors.

### *Three with a Two Wing (3w2)*

A Three with a Two wing is going to care about achieving in the context of relationships more than achieving outward success (like an average Three or 3w4). A Two's thoughtful nature can be a great addition to a Three's energy. The Enneagram Institute calls this wing type "the Charmer," and that's very accurate, as it's hard not to love a 3w2.

However, Threes with a Two wing have a hard time with emotions, as one of their greatest desires is to be independent of needing help from others. This need for independence causes a 3w2 to spin bad emotions or circumstances into a more positive light, similar to a Seven or a 6w7.

The tension this type struggles with is the tension between being efficient and helpful because when they have a draw to help people, it can be hard to say no and stay on task with what needs to be done.

### Three with a Four Wing (3w4)

A Four wing can bring beautiful creativity, a rich thought life, and emotional awareness to the life of a Three. Threes with a Four wing will often have a plethora of social charm, motivation to get stuff done, and a creative nature, making them fun to talk to as well as making them especially great entrepreneurs. However, when a Three is unhealthy, a Four wing will cause them to internalize criticism or negative information and scream, "You're a fake!" into their ears. Talk about tension! Threes with a Four wing who are not self-aware often face a long journey to fully appreciate and utilize their Four wing, but when they do, it's a beautiful thing.

## ARROWS

The arrows are the two numbers your Enneagram number is connected to in the Enneagram diagram. These two arrows represent the number from which you get the best traits as you grow, or the number from which you get the worst traits when you're in seasons of stress.

### Stress: Going to Nine

In stress, Threes will slow down and have little to no motivation as they behave like an unhealthy Nine. A Three in stress will indulge in mind-numbing behaviors, lose track of time, procrastinate on projects, and possibly even use passive-aggressive behavior to get someone's attention.

### Growth: Going to Six

In growth, Threes will become more in touch with their emotions and less competitive as they pick up the healthy behaviors of a Six. Secure Threes will care less about the illusion of others they need to impress and more about their close friends and family.

## TYPE THREE SUBTYPES

When we talk about subtypes and the Enneagram, we are referring to three relational instincts we all have. These instincts, like those of *fight or flight*, are reactions over which we have little control. The three relational subtypes are Self-Preservation (Sp), Social (So), and One-to-One (Sx). We all have the capacity to use all three of these instincts, but one of them is usually dominant. That dominant subtype can strongly impact how your distinct Enneagram type looks to the rest of us.

## The Efficient Three (Sp)

Self-preservation Threes are the least likely of all the three subtypes to boast in their strengths. They're the counter type Three. This Three wants to get things done without a lot of fuss and do things well for their own gratification, making them look very similar to an Enneagram One. Although they may not like it, these Threes would have to admit that their image is very important to them. These Threes might struggle with anxiety over their image and whether people like them.

## The "Best" Three (So)

The social subtype Three wants to provide for their team/ circle of influence by being an effective leader and making them all look good. This Three is very competitive and may get defensive in the face of criticism or failure. These Threes can easily read a room and adjust their persona accordingly. This subtype of Three is the least likely to mistype.

## The "Helper" Three (Sx)

The competitive nature of these Threes is usually aimed toward gaining affection or praise from those they love. They want to be the best, but if they don't like you (or you aren't close to them), they won't bat an eyelash if you don't like them. This subtype of Three is likely to mistype as a Two because they are very social and love to be helpful. Unlike a Two, however, usually their desire to be helpful is conditioned on how close they feel to the relationship.

# SO I'M A THREE. WHAT NOW?

**W**hy should I, as a type Three, embark on sixty days of devotions?

Whether you have just realized you are a type Three on the Enneagram or have already known that fact for some time, you've probably thought at one point, *Okay, but what now? I get that I'm an Achiever. I crave accomplishment, I dislike feeling unproductive or lacking, and I struggle with needing approval. The question is, how do I take this self-awareness and turn it into practical transformation?*

Some Enneagram teachers will tell you that you need only to focus on self-actualization and pull yourself up by your proverbial bootstraps to grow out of your worst behaviors. They say things like, "Meditate!" or "Focus on yourself!" or "You're perfect just the way you are, stop caring what people think!"

However, I'm here to offer a different foundation for growth. As Christians, we know that we are flawed, sinful, and far from God's intended plan for humanity. The hymn "Come Thou Fount of Every Blessing" includes the lyrics, "Prone to wander, Lord, I feel it." This speaks to the reality of our hearts and their rebellious nature toward our Savior.

This wandering is the problem, sin is the problem, we are the problem! So, anyone who tells us that we ought to focus on ourselves to find growth will only lead us to more confusion. We may even find ourselves back where we started, as we go around and around this idea of focusing on self.

But we are not without hope. Philippians 1:6 says, *"I am sure of this, that he who began a good work in you will bring it to completion at the day of Jesus Christ."* On the very day you acknowledged Jesus as your Savior, repented from your sin, and dedicated your life to Him, He began a good work in your life. This work is called sanctification, which is the act of becoming holy. Your sanctification will not be finished here on earth, but you are in the process of *becoming*, day by day, moment by moment, only by the Holy Spirit's work and power within you.

We might not know how to articulate it, but this work of sanctification is the growth and change for which we long. All of us know we are not who we want to be. Reflecting on the human condition in Romans 7:15, Paul says, *"For I do not understand my own actions. For I do not do what I want, but I do the very thing I hate."* Isn't that the truth? I don't want to care so much what people think of me, but here I am again.

We all know we have this haunting *potential* that always seems just a little out of reach. We all have this nagging feeling that we are created for more...but how do we get there? Only by God's grace and power within us can we rest in His sanctifying work and trust Him for the growth and potential of bringing glory to Him day by day. Only God can sanctify us, but it is our responsibility to be *"slaves of righteousness"* (Romans 6:18) and obey Him.

Over the next sixty days, we want to take you day by day through what God says about *your specific problems as a Three* and how He wants to lovingly sanctify you into being more like Jesus.

The lens of the Enneagram gives us a great starting point for your specific pain points and strengths. We will use those to encourage you in the areas that God is reflected through you and in the areas that you need to lay down your instincts and let Him change you.

Some of these topics might be hard, but we hope that you'll let the tension you feel in your heart open you up to change. This is where our obedience comes in. We all have blind spots and areas we are more comfortable leaving in the dark, but God desires so much more for us. So ask Him to help you release your grip on those areas, bring them into the light, and experience the freedom of repentance.

Hey! Look at me!
I'm a Three, and I can be
Anything I want to be!
Whether I'm loud or quiet, fast or slow,
I can change to fit the status quo.
To suit the need, you can count on me,
I just switch my personality.
Right from the start, the very beginning,
I was here to achieve, it's all about winning.
If you take me on, be prepared for a loss,
I'll always come first, whatever the cost.
I'll do what it takes, just watch and see,
No one ever gets one up on me.

But beneath it all, this sparkling skin
Hides secrets buried deep within.

Somewhere inside there's a little girl
Who's desperate to be valued in this world.
I'm afraid to find her, to call her name,
Because I know it will only reveal shame.
I can't let her be seen, can't let her show
Because then the real me you'll get to know.

So I'm loved for who I am, not what I do?
Let's take the plunge and see if it's true...

—*Ruth Addis*

# YOUR GUIDES FOR THIS JOURNEY

**Y**ou'll be hearing from two other writers and Enneagram coaches in the days ahead. The days in which no author is listed are written by me. On other days, I have asked an Enneagram Three and fellow Enneagram coach to help you on your path.

## JENA STAGNER

Jena is a 3w4 and Holistic Life coach whose mission in life is to help other ambitious women become unstoppable. She discovered the Enneagram three years ago and has been digging deep into it ever since.

Jena shares her perspective for several days in this devotional. She is passionate about self-development and living as a healthy Three. You will benefit greatly from her years of insight. Jena is an avid photographer and lives in Washington State with her husband and two dogs.

## ALISON BRADLEY

Alison is an Enneagram Nine who has always loved stories, whether it is reading them or helping others listen to their own. You'll often find her outside making a bouquet of flowers, or inside relaxing at the local library. She also loves being around her kitchen table in Bucks County, Pennsylvania, with her husband and two kids, often eating gluten-free chocolate chip pancakes.

# 10 DAYS OF ACTION
*How You Uniquely Reflect Christ*

## DAY 1 • • • • • • • • • • •

*What Is a Driven Nature?*

*The people who know their God shall stand firm and take action.*
(Daniel 11:32)

Enneagram Threes are defined by their driven nature. The word *driven* means "highly energetic and motivated." This is often misunderstood as meaning outgoing or extroverted, but in the Enneagram context, it's understood as expending energy toward accomplishing tasks, being self-motivated, and taking action.

Don't get me wrong—a lot of Threes are indeed extroverts or are very outgoing in social situations, but you don't have to be an extrovert to be a type Three. Having energy for tasks and being highly motivated often makes Threes gifted at planning for the future, getting things done, and casting vision. This is a huge asset in professional fields but also is a great quality in any friend, spouse, or parent.

Threes' drive helps them make a tangible impact on the world, and when living in fellowship with God, they become some of the most celebrated pillars of our faith, building others up, spreading the gospel, planting churches, writing books, preaching, teaching, shepherding, and accomplishing much in the name of Christ.

---

## SHIFT IN FOCUS

In the Bible, the closest word we find to what we mean by *driven* or *drive* is *action*, so we will use those words similarly in the days ahead. Daniel 11:32 speaks of a firm and active faith. Often we can be tempted to have an active faith without knowledge, where we are *"tossed to and fro by the waves and carried about by every wind of doctrine"* (Ephesians 4:14). Or we can have a firm faith full of knowledge but fail to actually act on our faith.

*So also faith by itself, if it does not have works, is dead.*

(James 2:17)

It honors God when we know what we believe, stand firm in those beliefs, *and* take action.

How does your driven nature as a Three help you with this?

Do you find yourself prone to act without knowledge or have knowledge without action?

# DAY 2 • • • • • • • • • • • •

## How We All Reflect God

*And let the peace of Christ rule in your hearts,*
*to which indeed you were called in one body.*
(Colossians 3:15)

Dear Achiever, did you know you uniquely reflect God? In Genesis 1:26–27, God says He made us in His image. Now, this doesn't mean our bodies look like His, but we reflect His image by reflecting parts of God's character. It's not a perfect reflection; in fact, it's rippled and marred. However, a familiarity, a family resemblance, is still plainly evident between God and His creation.

God is so mighty, majestic, and perfect that none of us can reflect every part of Him, so we see His attributes scattered throughout the entire population. Each and every one of us is reflecting Him in unique and very important ways. This is why we hear about each of us being a part of God's *body*. (See 1 Corinthians 12:27; Romans 12:5; Ephesians 5:30.) Each of us is uniquely made for a divine purpose; each of us is not wholly effective without the others.

As a Three, you reflect God's action, His excellence, His establishing, and His inspiring and encouraging nature as you grow in sanctification. God made you uniquely, specifically, and purposefully. Your drive might get you places, but it ultimately reflects God.

Your desire to see people thrive, the way you easily encourage, or your tendency toward action may feel second nature to you as a Three, especially as you are following Christ. But these are all important ways you uniquely reflect God to those around you.

---

## SHIFT IN FOCUS

Did you grow up hearing that you shared physical resemblances with anyone? Similar quirks?

As you go about your day, invite God to reveal the ways He's made you to look like Him. If you have space, pull out a journal and think of things you've noticed about yourself or heard others say about your drive, excellence, or ability to inspire, encourage, or understand. God can help you notice these parts of who you are. Thank Him for choosing you and calling you holy and beloved. Invite Him to continue to grow you as an Achiever who looks like Him.

# DAY 3 • • • • • • • • • • •

How Threes Reflect God

*So God created man in his own image, in the image of God he created him; male and female he created them.*
(Genesis 1:27)

Threes tend to be social, active, and driven, so your reflection of God isn't a quiet one. This is both good and bad because, when you're living for Christ, you have the potential to bring many eyes to Him. But when you're living for yourself, you can quickly burn out and become weighed down by the expectations that accompany pride. It can be so tempting to pursue self-glory instead of glory for Christ because vanity is satisfying in the moment, but it does not deliver on what it promises.

Long-lasting joy, hope, fulfillment, and peace are ultimately found in Christ. When you give glory to Him for your talents, gifts, and the praise you receive, He will truly satisfy the longings of your heart.

But what are specific ways Threes reflect God, and what do those look like? You reflect God with your love of excellence, action, and efficiency, as well as with your talents in establishing, encouraging, and inspiring. Here is what these words mean as reflections of God:

**Excellence:** As you pursue excellence in your work and everyday life, you're reflecting God's love of excellence.

**Establishing:** You have a natural ability to see the potential in almost anything. This helps you to cast vision, encourage, and help fuel to action things that might have never moved forward on their own. God is the ultimate establisher, as He not only created us but established families, governments, prophets, and ultimately His plan to redeem humanity by sending His Son. God has a long vision for us and sees the potential in His creation.

**Encourager:** Having a natural bent toward seeing potential also helps you be an amazing encourager. The Holy Spirit is said to be our encourager, and your gifting here is a reflection of that part of God. (See John 14:16–17.)

**Inspiring:** Being gifted in encouraging, pursuing excellence, and taking action is the perfect recipe for being inspiring. The way you inspire can't hold a candle to the way God is inspiring, but even the small amount you reflect is enough to bring glory to Him.

**Action:** The opposite of laziness is action, and your action reflects our God, who never sleeps and whose action holds the world together.

**Efficiency:** As you do things with excellence, you also don't want to waste any time. This is where efficiency comes in, and your love of efficiency reflects our God, who does everything with an excellence and efficiency that we will never quite understand.

---

## SHIFT IN FOCUS

Spend some time in prayer thanking God for how you get to reflect His character to the world around you. If these words reflect your heart, please borrow them:

> Dear heavenly Father, I am in awe of the honor it is to reflect who You are. I thank You for giving me gifts from Your very heart, and I pray that You would keep my heart pure and focused on You as I use them. Give me a grateful heart toward my talents as I am reminded that they were never mine to begin with. Help me to point others toward You, and help me to grow more and more humble every day. Amen.

• • • • • • • • • • • **DAY 4**

*God's Action*

*Thus says God, the LORD, who created the heavens and stretched them out, who spread out the earth and what comes from it, who gives breath to the people on it and spirit to those who walk in it.*
(Isaiah 42:5)

**D**ear Achiever, what is the picture of God you have in your head? I think we all picture God a little differently, but a lot of us picture Him in heaven—either watching the earth, reveling in praises, or maybe lounging while everyone serves Him. This picture is what causes us to struggle to think of God as a God of action. Maybe we'd concede that God was more active during Old Testament times, but He certainly doesn't seem so active today. However, this is a wrong assumption.

All three parts of the Trinity are described as beings of action:

**God** did not create, then leave. He has not lost the motivation to continue to be active in every minute detail of the earth. He created, He planned, He redeemed, and He is still creating, fulfilling His plans, and redeeming His creation.

God does not sleep, God does not stop, and God does not need to rest. In Genesis, when He took a day of rest after creating the earth, He did so as an example to us—not because He Himself was tired or needed to rest.

**Jesus** is said to be at God's right hand interceding for us. As Romans 8:34 says, *"Who is to condemn? Christ Jesus is the one who died—more than that, who was raised—who is at the right hand of God, who indeed is interceding for us."* Interceding is not an inactive word. It means to negotiate, beg, plead, or pray. While He is in heaven, before He returns, Jesus is active for our benefit, protection, and good.

**The Holy Spirit** is described as a teacher, reminder, and supporter to us in our daily lives. As John 14:26 states, *"But the Helper, the Holy Spirit, whom the Father will send in my name, he will teach you all things and bring to your remembrance all that I have said to you."* The Holy Spirit is active in a supporting role to God's people.

---

## SHIFT IN FOCUS

Does your view of God, Jesus, and the Holy Spirit reflect the kind of action we see ascribed to them in Scripture?

Do you tend to picture the Trinity as They acted during Bible times, or do you picture Them in their roles right now in your life?

As you have read of your own reflection of God's image having a great deal to do with action, how does reading about God's current action encourage you?

• • • • • • • • • • • •  **DAY 5**

*Action in the Bible*

*So Gideon took ten men of his servants and did as the Lord had told him. But because he was too afraid of his family and the men of the town to do it by day, he did it by night.*

(Judges 6:27)

The Bible is full of stories of action, both of God and His people. A lot of these action stories are of war, some are of love, but most of the action revolves around people trusting God when they didn't understand why He was asking them to act. Three examples of these stories in the Bible are those of Abraham, Gideon, and Jonah, but these three men have drastically different degrees of faith that impacted their action.

## ACTION IN FAITH

God had a strange request for Abraham:

*He said, "Take your son, your only son Isaac, whom you love, and go to the land of Moriah, and offer him there as a burnt offering on one of the mountains of which I shall tell you."*  (Genesis 22:2)

We don't know exactly why God asked this of Abraham. Nevertheless, Abraham obeyed and acted. By faith, he bound his only son and put him on the altar as a sacrifice, foreshadowing what would happen to God's own Son in the New Testament.

God stopped Abraham before Isaac was harmed, and He praised Abraham for his faith.

## HESITANT ACTION IN FAITH

We hear the story of Gideon in Judges 6–7. Gideon is known as one of the greatest judges of the Old Testament, yet he was a hesitant leader. Gideon asked for signs from God, he hid, he snuck around, and he tried to make himself comfortable with a big army that God pared down to just three hundred men. Gideon *did* act when all was said and done, but his hesitance was a sign of his lack of faith. God upped the stakes of Gideon's faith again and again until his faith in God was all he had left when he faced the Midianites. His faith was rewarded by victory in battle, but the journey was a hard one because of his hesitance.

## ACTION IN DISBELIEF

The book of Jonah is the tale of a prophet who tried to run from God. Jonah was a man of action, but his action was characterized by disbelief in God. God told Jonah to go to the city of Nineveh and preach to those people, but Jonah did not want to go; he didn't think the people of Nineveh were worthy of God's mercy.

> But Jonah rose to flee to Tarshish from the presence of the LORD. He went down to Joppa and found a ship going to Tarshish. So he paid the fare and went down into it, to go with them to Tarshish, away from the presence of the LORD. (Jonah 1:3)

Do you relate to one of these examples more than the other two? With God's help, you can be emboldened to choose action in faith! And in His faithfulness, God is still right here, even when you struggle to choose faith or when you need help picking up the pieces.

## SHIFT IN FOCUS

In our lives, we will see all three of these stories play out in different ways. We all have times of action in faith, hesitant action in faith, and action in disbelief. Pinpoint and write down an example from your own life of these three types of action.

Action in faith:

_____

_____

_____

Hesitant action in faith:

_____

_____

_____

Action in disbelief:

_____

_____

_____

# DAY 6 • • • • • • • • • • • •

## Action and Obedience
### By Jena Stagner

*For we are his workmanship, created in Christ Jesus for good works, which God prepared beforehand, that we should walk in them.* (Ephesians 2:10)

You most likely ask yourself, "What should I do?" multiple times throughout the day. You may even have numerous lists from which you could choose an answer to that question.

Maybe you already took the time to build your schedule for the day, and you're ready to act, or you're overwhelmed by all the actions you could take. Regardless of the circumstance, you long for action and look to take the right steps every day because fulfilling your dreams and ambitions requires a lot of action.

So how do you know that what you're doing is what you *should* be doing?

Obedience.

Obedience is not what we should do. Because as we see in Ephesians 2:10, God knows what we are to do: the good works He already prepared for us to walk in. There is no standard or expectation according to which God is criticizing your action. He simply calls for your obedience to the actions He already created for you.

He created these right actions so that you would walk in them. There is no need to figure it all out or make sure it's perfect;

you simply need to walk out the day in obedience to what God has already prepared for you.

As you look through your life, consider the actions you are planning to take and how God sees them. Are they in alignment with the good works He has prepared for you in advance?

If shame creeps in, consider how your actions may only exist because of someone else's standards and expectations of what you should do, and not from obedience to God and the good works He prepared for you. Living to meet others' standards and expectations will always leave us burdened by an impossible demand.

The actions to take already exist within the right action of obedience, which is always good works.

Let's redefine our to-do list, seeing it instead as a good-works list, a list of right actions already prepared that are calling for our obedience. No longer living from the burden of "should" that others give us, but for the life of good works God prepared for us in advance.

That drive for good works is a holy calling. And it's only through our faith that we can take the steps of obedience. So today, let's be characterized by faith in action, fulfilling the good works God prepared for us in advance.

---

## SHIFT IN FOCUS

What on your agenda or to-do list today has you most excited?

Do you see these actions as good works God prepared beforehand?

Is there anything you're dreading or that doesn't feel like a good work?

Is this due to an area of disobedience? How can you shift that from drudgery to delight?

What are some good works God is calling you to do that haven't made it onto your agenda or list?

# • • • • • • • • • • • • DAY 7

## Holy Ambition vs. Selfish Ambition
### By Jena Stagner

*The point is this: whoever sows sparingly will also reap sparingly, and whoever sows bountifully will also reap bountifully. Each one must give as he has decided in his heart, not reluctantly or under compulsion, for God loves a cheerful giver. And God is able to make all grace abound to you, so that having all sufficiency in all things at all times, you may abound in every good work.*
(2 Corinthians 9:6–8)

Dear Achiever, yesterday we looked at your right actions as faithful obedience to God and doing the good works He prepared for you in advance. As you take action, you might find yourself judging whether your motives are pure or based on selfish ambition.

Because Threes are in the heart triad, meaning shame is our core emotion, this judgment quickly leads to shame when we believe our ambition is what's wrong with us.

If we look in the *Oxford English Dictionary*, we see ambition defined as: "A strong desire to do or to achieve something, require determination and hard work."

Ambition is not what's wrong with us. Good works require holy ambition.

In today's focus verse, we see that our God desires abundance when it comes to good works. And James 2:26 tells us, "*Faith apart from works is dead.*"

God desires us to do all the good we possibly can, and this requires ambition.

We shift from holy ambition to selfish ambition when we no longer operate from our true identity, take our eyes off of reflecting God and His grace, and believe we have the ability and strength to make it all work.

We become driven to get it right for our name rather than getting it done in Jesus's name.

God wants our big ambitions, but only when they are in alignment with His. Right action takes a level of surrender and faith that doesn't always look like what we might consider to be good or perfect. Quite often, the way God calls us to follow doesn't make sense to our selfish ambition.

What is God's ambition for your life?

*In the same way, let your light shine before others, so that they may see your good works and give glory to your Father who is in heaven.* (Matthew 5:16)

Said another way, God's ambition is for you to do good works for others and give God the glory.

Every action must come from a faithful step of obedience, or your selfish ambition will be there to take the stage. This temptation will always be there.

It's not about going through life perfectly doing good work in the absence of selfish ambition; rather, it is about being someone who is on alert for when selfish ambition wants to take over and surrendering that desire in Jesus's name.

---

## SHIFT IN FOCUS

Is there something in your life that is motivated by selfish ambition?

Spend some time in prayer asking God what His ambition is for this area of your life.

What practices could you create to help you develop a rhythm of assessing your actions to see if selfish ambition is there?

Spend some time connecting with what it takes to live with holy ambition as you pursue the good works God has prepared for you.

What does this look like in your life from a practical and tangible perspective?

# DAY 8 • • • • • • • • • • •

Action vs. Reaction

*Now Peter was sitting outside in the courtyard. And a servant girl came up to him and said, "You also were with Jesus the Galilean." But he denied it before them all, saying, "I do not know what you mean." And when he went out to the entrance, another servant girl saw him, and she said to the bystanders, "This man was with Jesus of Nazareth." And again he denied it with an oath: "I do not know the man." After a little while the bystanders came up and said to Peter, "Certainly you too are one of them, for your accent betrays you." Then he began to invoke a curse on himself and to swear, "I do not know the man." And immediately the rooster crowed. And Peter remembered the saying of Jesus, "Before the rooster crows, you will deny me three times." And he went out and wept bitterly.* (Matthew 26:69–75)

Peter, Jesus's disciple, was a man of action. He left his livelihood to follow Jesus, he was the only disciple to step out of the boat and walk on the water to Jesus, he wrote at least two books of the Bible, and Jesus proclaimed him to be the cornerstone of the early church: *"And I tell you, you are Peter, and on this rock I will build my church, and the gates of hell shall not prevail against it"* (Matthew 16:18).

But Peter was also a man of *reaction*—an action performed or a feeling experienced in response to a situation or event—and this got him into a lot of trouble. As Jesus was being arrested, Peter rose to the Lord's defense and cut off a guard's ear with his sword. (See John 18:10.) Peter rebuked Jesus when He foretold His death. (See Mark 8:31–33.) And in the verses for today, we read of Peter's denial of Christ. We know this is a reaction because Peter had told Jesus just hours earlier that he would never deny Him. But Peter was scared and overwhelmed; he reacted with what must've felt like the best social decision at the time.

When you're a person of action, you have to guard yourself against these types of reactions. Not all reactions are wrong or cause harm, but many do—and it takes humility to assume that you need to keep your reactions in check.

When do you see yourself doing the most reacting? Is it when you face strong peer pressure? When you're protecting those you love? When you find yourself in a leadership role and you're trying to be proactive? The easiest way to find out is to ask yourself, *When was the last time I did something I regretted, and what was the circumstance?* Identifying when you tend to do most of your reacting will help you to identify those moments as they are happening and give you the space to think, consider emotions (both your own and others), and use self-control if necessary.

Self-control is a fruit of the Spirit, and God can help grow that fruit in you. Ask Him to help you be proactive before you go into situations that cause you to become emotional, and celebrate your baby steps of growth.

---

## SHIFT IN FOCUS

Like Peter, you may be a person of action who also has a tendency to *react*.

Name three ways being prone to action helps you:

_____

_____

_____

Name three reactions you regret:

_____

_____

_____

● ● ● ● ● ● ● ● ● ● ● **DAY 9**

Action When God Says No
By Jena Stagner

*I will remember the deeds of the* LORD; *yes,*
*I will remember your wonders of old.*
*I will ponder all your work, and meditate on your mighty deeds.*
(Psalm 77:11–12)

Dear Achiever, you do not lack passion for what matters to you; at times, you may even be relentless when you want something to go a certain way. But what about those moments when, no matter what action you could take, you can't change the outcome?

Maybe it's a failed relationship, infertility, or the loss of a loved one. Or perhaps it's the desire for a career change or a new business idea that no longer seems like it's for you.

What is the right action when God says "no" to our dream, wish, or desire?

Surrendering, trusting, and having faith may seem like the most obvious answers to that question, but God does give us an action we can take in the face of disappointment or devastation. He calls us to biblical lament: being honest with Him about our grief or sorrow when life seems hard and our burdens feel heavy.

Four elements characterize biblical lament:

## 1. CONNECTING WITH GOD

Drawing closer and not pulling away or taking things into your own hands when you face disappointment or devastation.

## 2. AUTHENTIC EXPRESSION

Sharing your true feelings, knowing God can handle them all. There is no need to look good or have the perfect answer with God, so express yourself fully and authentically.

## 3. HONEST REQUEST

Making your true desires known to God. There is no perfect answer, but you can ask God honestly for what you desire, connected to your most genuine desire, or express what you would like to change to have your life go a different way.

## 4. FAITHFUL SURRENDER

Giving up the need to do anything or have anything change and trusting God to lead the way. When you've poured out how you truly feel and what you desire, surrendering is your next right action.

If you are still holding onto something, the last step may feel impossible. Refocus your thoughts to determine why this is so, and begin with the first step again. Continue until you can reach the place of faithful surrender.

It's easy for Threes to set aside feelings in order to tackle whatever needs to get done, so this call to biblical lament may not come naturally. It's okay if it takes some work. It is good to work to connect with the One who is in ultimate control.

Be open to being moved by your greatest desires and the loss you feel when God says no. We see this powerfully expressed in the Psalms.

We may want to find a way around genuinely feeling what's there for us. But if God says no, there is purpose in that. We may not understand it or know what to do—and that's the gift of biblical lament.

---

## SHIFT IN FOCUS

Give yourself the space to focus on what you genuinely feel today. Consider an area of your life where you feel disappointment or devastation and work through the biblical lament process.

The connection to emotion may not come easily, so think of biblical lament as the next right action to take amid the hard things of life.

This process isn't about getting it right or getting it done, but opening your heart and allowing God to take you on the journey of casting all your burdens on Him.

*Cast your burden on the LORD, and he will sustain you; he will never permit the righteous to be moved.* (Psalm 55:22)

# DAY 10 • • • • • • • • • •

*Action That Requires Faith*
*By Jena Stagner*

*For my thoughts are not your thoughts,*
*neither are your ways my ways, declares the LORD.*
*For as the heavens are higher than the earth, so are my ways higher*
*than your ways and my thoughts than your thoughts.*
(Isaiah 55:8–9)

All actions God calls you to will always require faith because God's plan is bigger than your plan. His ways are beyond your ways, and you need your faith in order to connect with that.

With your drive and ambition, getting things done may be simple for you, but along with that is the temptation to depend on your own strength. There is no escaping this. As with every action, you have a choice—a choice to take action as a step of faithful obedience or a step out of trusting in our own strength.

There will always be the temptation to take the easy way. And when it comes to getting things done, the drive to complete the task can be stronger than the drive to connect with God's purpose.

You may see the project, but God sees His purpose.

Faithful action may be an area of weakness for you, but avoid going into shame here. This insufficiency is a space where you get to uniquely and powerfully connect with God.

*But he said to me, "My grace is sufficient for you, for my power is made perfect in weakness." Therefore I will boast all the more gladly of my weaknesses, so that the power of Christ may rest upon me.* (2 Corinthians 12:9)

There is no need to hide this weakness; let it be as it is. Recognize that you need God's grace here, not your perfection. Then, after surrendering your need to be perfect, take the faithful action that is there for you and act from a place of obedience.

When you disconnect with this, connect with God's grace again, and recommit yourself to reflecting God's glory.

---

## SHIFT IN FOCUS

With the temptation to feel shame, see where you may be more connected with perfection than God's grace. In what area of life do you see the drive to be perfect over being faithful?

Faithful action has space to try and fail. Perfect action doesn't have room to be human. Who we are is not a surprise to God. He knows our temptations, and He has fully redeemed us. He has made a way based not on our action, but on His Son's.

There are no actions required to receive God's grace. Jesus did all the work. God desires you to be effective beyond what you can see. He desires for you to be effective in the thoughts and ways that are higher than yours, reflecting His glory to the world.

# 10 DAYS OF KILLING DECEIT

How the Enemy Wants You to Stop Reflecting God

## DAY 11 • • • • • • • • • • •

*What Is a Deadly Sin?*

*If anyone is caught in any transgression,*
*you who are spiritual should restore him in a spirit of gentleness.*
*Keep watch on yourself, lest you too be tempted.*
(Galatians 6:1)

**A**lthough the wording or specific idea for the "seven deadly sins" is not in the Bible, the list of them has been used by Christians for ages. The classification of seven deadly sins that we know today was first penned by a monk named Evagrius Ponticus who lived from AD 345–399.

This list has gone through many changes since its origination, but it has remained a helpful way for us to name the common vices that keep us in chains.

When these seven sins are paired with specific Enneagram numbers (plus two extra sins to make nine), they give us a better idea of the specific vices that may be tripping us up again and again. This is important because these problems are often blind spots in our lives. Their exposure leads us to repentance, better health, and greater unity with Christ, which is the greatest thing learning about our Enneagram number can do for us.

Here are the deadly sins early Enneagram teachers paired with each type:

1. Anger
2. Pride
3. Deceit
4. Envy
5. Greed
6. Fear
7. Gluttony
8. Lust
9. Sloth

Struggling with one of these sins dominantly does not mean that you do not struggle with all of them. If we are honest with ourselves and humble, we can all recognize ourselves in each of the sins listed. However, your dominant deadly sin is a specific tool Satan will use to distract the world from seeing how you reflect God.

For Threes, the deadly sin you struggle with most is deceit, and whether or not you recognize deceit in your own life as you're thinking about it now, I entreat you to give great thought to it in these next ten days.

Exposing blind spots in our life can feel a lot like ripping off a bandage that we might prefer to leave on, but what's underneath is God-honoring and beautiful.

---

## SHIFT IN FOCUS

Spend some time contemplating and praying about what deceit might look like in your life.

What does that word actually mean when you look it up?

Does it surprise you to see that specific sin printed next to your Enneagram type?

• • • • • • • • • • • • **DAY 12**

*What Is Deceit?*

*Put off your old self, which belongs to your former manner of life and is corrupt through deceitful desires.*
(Ephesians 4:22)

The word *deceit* means the action or practice of deceiving someone by concealing or misrepresenting the truth. When we think of deceit, we tend to fixate on the lie—what it is or whether it's a big deal. But deceit actually has very little to do with the lie and everything to do with what the truth is. To misrepresent something is often easier than we realize.

Misrepresenting the truth can be as simple as rounding up your GPA just a little. Misrepresenting the truth is giving advice and letting people assume you follow that advice yourself, even if you don't. You can misrepresent the truth without even saying a word, by merely failing to correct someone's false assumption. All of these misrepresentations can be so tempting!

However, telling what we might call a *white lie* or remaining silent when someone expresses a falsehood is still deceit. If you habitually misrepresent the truth, at some point, you'll get caught, and when that happens, your encouraging and inspiring reflection of God loses its credibility.

In some cases, Threes who are especially unhealthy and make a living out of misrepresenting the truth in order to make others happy lose their leadership position, friends, families, careers, and more. Much like Anakin Skywalker and his fall to the dark side, the very things that unhealthy Threes deceive in order to protect will ultimately be the casualties of their deceit. How tragically ironic.

God doesn't call us to engage in honesty out of fun, but because deceit is toxic and will destroy everything in its path if we let it grow in our lives.

---

## SHIFT IN FOCUS

Spend some time asking God to expose areas of your life where you tend to misrepresent the truth.

What are you trying to accomplish by not speaking the whole truth?

Is there someone to whom you need to come clean?

## • • • • • • • • • • • • DAY 13

### Why Is Deceit a Three's Deadly Sin?

*For am I now seeking the approval of man, or of God?*
*Or am I trying to please man? If I were still trying to please man,*
*I would not be a servant of Christ.*
(Galatians 1:10)

Hearing the word *deceit* in correlation to your personality might send you into full defense mode—and understandably so. After all, it was deceit that Satan used in the garden of Eden to cause the fall of mankind. As serious as deceit is, I understand why Threes get a bit defensive about seeing this word next to their Enneagram type.

I've had Threes get hurt, defensive, angry, and even unfollow me on social media for teaching that deceit is type Three's deadly sin. I get it—this is a touchy topic.

You may be thinking, *But I never purposefully lie to people! Deceitful is never a word I'd use to describe myself! I pride myself on being honest and open with others.*

All these things may be true. However, I'd like to propose that if you replace the word *deceit* with the phrase *people-pleasing*, it may feel a bit more accurate. Through my interviews with type Threes, I've come to understand that Threes do not *normally* intentionally deceive people, but rather they form a habit of misrepresenting themselves in order to please others and come across as more confident than they are. Even if this is not malicious, others may never know about it, and it's still somewhat socially acceptable, this is still deceit.

Here's something a Three once told me: "I'm so painfully socially aware that it doesn't occur to me to correct others' even subtle assumptions about me. I think I do this to avoid conflict and prevent disappointing those around me."

Dear Achiever, your heart is so tender toward people that sometimes you may try to be what they want you to be, even if you're not. This is why your deceit doesn't always feel gross, ugly, or harmful. Sometimes your deceit feels like how you love. However, you don't need to hide who you are in order to love others. That is a lie straight from Satan.

## SHIFT IN FOCUS

How does the word *deceit* make you feel?

Does the phrase *people-pleaser* make more sense?

Do you struggle with believing the lie that you need to hide who you are in order to love others?

## • • • • • • • • • • DAY 14

*But I Don't Do That!*

> *These are the things that you shall do: Speak the truth to one another; render in your gates judgments that are true and make for peace; do not devise evil in your hearts against one another, and love no false oath, for all these things I hate, declares the LORD.*
> (Zechariah 8:16–17)

Hearing how people-pleasing is a way you love others and how deceit might be much more discreet than you initially perceived might help you to recognize its impact in your life. However, from my experience talking to Threes, I know that you still might not be convinced that the people-pleasing you do is lying. So here's an example:

Imagine someone you're getting to know at work or church starts talking about their love of a famous movie or book franchise that you think is overrated. You don't voice your true opinion about it. Instead, you nod and smile while they talk about their favorite scenes, how the movies compare to the books, and other remarks of that nature. When they ask if you want to come to their annual extended-edition marathon, you're conflicted internally, thinking, *I definitely do not want to spend an entire day watching the movie franchise, but it feels so awkward to say that. Plus, I'm trying to build a relationship with this person. I'll just say I'd love to go, then something will "come up."*

So you agree to go, even though you have no intention of actually going. Or maybe you just say, "That sounds cool!"

without actually agreeing to go but also not being open about your decision to avoid it.

Most of the clients I've presented this scenario to have said that this would not necessarily be lying. They've argued that dumping on someone's favorite franchise is rude, so they'd have a clear conscience just letting the conversation go on without mentioning their true feelings.

However, if this new acquaintance were to tell one of your friends that you agreed to come to their movie marathon, what if your friend reacted by saying, "What? They hate that franchise! I've heard them rant about its over-popularity at least a dozen times." If this were to happen, you would be caught in a lie.

When you go through most of your life people-pleasing and believing your 100 percent truest self will not always be welcome, it can seem like the only two options left are to misrepresent the truth or be rude. However, there is a third option here. You can say, "I've never met someone so into this franchise! It's not really for me, but I admire your passion for it." This is just one of a slew of polite yet honest phrases.

It's true that some people might get offended even when you disagree with them politely, but that doesn't mean that you did something wrong. You're more in trouble with God for misrepresenting the truth than for not making everyone happy 100 percent of the time. That is not your calling.

—————————————————

## SHIFT IN FOCUS

Do you feel pressure to make others happy, even if that means you can't always be honest?

Reflect on the reading from Zechariah. What is it telling you *to do*, and what is it telling you *not to do*?

# DAY 15 • • • • • • • • • •

*People-Pleasing and Deception for Others' Good*

*But just as we have been approved by God to be entrusted*
*with the gospel, so we speak, not to please man,*
*but to please God who tests our hearts.*
(1 Thessalonians 2:4)

God wants us to focus on pleasing Him and not man for a couple of key reasons:

1.  God is the only source of true and lasting joy, peace, comfort, and salvation.

2.  People are fickle, and pleasing them is a fruitless endeavor.

I see this so often as my heart aches to please mankind. It causes me anxiety because I can't please everyone, and no matter what choice I make or what I say, I could offend someone.

God's call for us to please Him and not man is not Him being dictatorial or exerting His power. Rather, it is a sign of His care for us. God wants us to focus on what matters and not waste our precious days on chasing the wind of popular opinion. He is championing for us to live without anxiety and fear of man.

You may know that "Jenny" only listens to Christian music, but you listen to multiple genres without conviction. If you carpool with her, don't just turn on your local Christian radio station and let her assume that's all you listen to. Don't change what you normally do. Instead, have a conversation. You can tell her that this is what you listen to but you'll change the station if it makes her uncomfortable. You don't need to lie or change who you are to be kind, loving, or considerate. All you need is to own what you and God have worked out together, and be willing to have semi-difficult or even hard conversations.

First Corinthians 13:6 says that love *"rejoices with the truth."* Where there is love, there is no room for misrepresenting the truth because love rejoices in the truth. When others get upset because the truth is being told, you can plainly see that there was no love to begin with.

## SHIFT IN FOCUS

Spend some time praying and journaling through these prompts:

+ Where or on what topic am I most tempted toward people-pleasing?

+ What does love *"rejoices with the truth"* mean practically for me today?

+ What does pleasing God look like for me today?

# DAY 16 • • • • • • • • • • •

*Protecting Your Image*

*Whatever you do, work heartily, as for the Lord and not for men.*
(Colossians 3:23)

**D**ear Achiever, what is the image you want people to see in their head when they think of you? Do you want them to see a talented entrepreneur, the best speaker they've ever heard, a loving husband, someone whose kids excel, a godly grandmother, or maybe a professional athlete? A quick look at your social media might shed some light on how you want to be seen. What hashtags do you use? What does your bio say? What kind of influencers and companies do you follow? What does all of this say about you and how you want to be seen?

Threes can get caught up in the temptation of deceit, especially when it comes to protecting their image. All of the heart triad (Twos, Threes, and Fours) are considered to be image-conscious, which means it's easy for them to see themselves how others may see them and they tend to want others to think well of them. It comes naturally for them to people-please, and they tend to be good at it.

You may have thought that ability or feeling was universal, but it's not something everyone has.

For Threes, this can be a double-edged sword because you're motivated by worth—both your self-worth and the value you can add to the world around you. Your worth gets so caught up in what you consider to be your identity or image that you may be misrepresenting the truth to protect it or to make that image just a little shinier.

The voice of deceit says, "They won't like you if they know you're too busy to take that on. Just say you have time and figure it out later." Or maybe it says, "If they really knew your GPA, they wouldn't be very impressed with you. Just tell them it's a couple points higher; nobody here *really* knows." Or maybe, "If they know you resent your childhood, then they won't see you as a *good Christian*. Maybe saying you had a great childhood, even if that's not the whole truth, is what forgiveness looks like anyway."

Protecting your image can look like extreme dieting, sacrificing your family on the altar of career, trading in loyal friends for people everyone likes, shifting the blame when you make mistakes, buying things you can't afford, or practicing deceit.

## SHIFT IN FOCUS

What would it mean for you to *"work heartily, as for the Lord and not for men"*?

We often feel that if people are happy with us, then God must be happy too, so we justify working for man's applause. But God wants your identity to be in Him as a new creation who is forgiven, loved, and wholly devoted to Christ. Anything and everything else should be pennies compared to the richness of the gift of salvation and your new life in Christ. The car you drive doesn't matter, what so-and-so thinks of you doesn't matter, your job title doesn't matter. If you're in Christ, then your worth has already been established. You cannot add to it, and you cannot take away from it.

Memorize Colossians 3:23.

# DAY 17 • • • • • • • • • • • •

*Deceit in the Bible*
*By Jena Stagner*

*Watch out for those who cause divisions and create obstacles*
*contrary to the doctrine that you have been taught.…For such*
*persons do not serve our Lord Christ, but their own appetites, and*
*by smooth talk and flattery they deceive the hearts of the naive.*
(Romans 16:17–18)

**D**eceit may not be the first thing you think of when you think about the Bible, but it's mentioned more than 160 times! You don't have to read too many pages before you reach the first devastating impact of deceit.

It's easy to minimize how serious deceit is, but even that in itself is deceitful. Misrepresenting the truth is powerful—and dangerous.

In Genesis 3:1, the serpent deceived Eve by asking, *"Did God actually say,"* knowing full well He said nothing of the sort. In doing so, he influenced Eve to choose sin. The very nature of the entire human race now defaults to sin due to Eve's choice and Adam's dismissal of responsibility.

While this example of deceit might not relate to where you find yourself today, there is a good chance you've misrepresented even the basic things in your life, like your schedule, care, or attention to those you care about most.

Until you get to the root of the inauthenticity, which is deceit, you impact your life in a way that can eventually lead to spiritual death. It may seem harmless at the moment, but the impact of deceit always grows.

You must repent and begin to take action in a new way, or you'll profoundly impact your life and others. Any workaround to this will delay resolution. There is no getting away with misrepresenting the truth.

God sees and knows—but He's not an angry Father.

In the case of Adam and Eve, God takes all the steps necessary to restore their wholeness. God wants you to see and know the impact of sin so that you can live fully restored and alive.

You have limitations, and you must live in light of this. Authenticity is hard for a Three, but when we misrepresent any aspect of ourselves or our life to the world around us, it only leads to more difficulty.

Instead, choose radical honesty and live fully connected to God and His abundant blessings for you in your life with your limitations. He desires you to live free from the stress and anxiety of trying to carry all the burdens of life perfectly.

---

## SHIFT IN FOCUS

Look at an area of your life where you feel stress or anxiety. In what ways might you be misrepresenting the truth in this area? Who have you been deceiving?

What would it look like for you to live fully authentic in this area? Repent of your deceit and choose an authentic step of faith in this area. You may not resolve the whole situation today, but begin to restore integrity in this area and take responsibility for the impact your deception has created.

Every weakness is an opportunity to see God more clearly in your life.

As you walk out radical honesty, you will express your most authentic self. If you feel terrified, consider what deception you believe in this area of your life.

In this space of authenticity, there is life.

## • • • • • • • • • • • DAY 18

### A Call to Radical Honesty
### By Jena Stagner

*Judge not, that you be not judged. For with the judgment you pronounce you will be judged, and with the measure you use it will be measured to you. Why do you see the speck that is in your brother's eye, but do not notice the log that is in your own eye? Or how can you say to your brother, "Let me take the speck out of your eye," when there is the log in your own eye? You hypocrite, first take the log out of your own eye, and then you will see clearly to take the speck out of your brother's eye.*
(Matthew 7:1–5)

**Y**esterday we examined where you might be misrepresenting the truth. Maybe it's in your career, at home, or even with yourself. Wherever it might be, walking out your calling to radical honesty will be what empowers you to walk out obedience in this area.

It's easy to think speaking the truth will only cause more problems. Or maybe you're in the middle of a circumstance that feels entirely impossible, so speaking the truth would accomplish nothing.

The distinction between radical honesty and speaking the truth is intention. When you desire what God wants, radical honesty always works. When you desire what you want, your ambition and ego get in the way, leading you to speak not *the* truth but *your* truth.

Jesus reflects the call to radical honesty. He fully surrendered to the Father's will, so He always made choices in alignment with that and never once was deceitful.

When Jesus was radically honest, He connected with people as they were right where they were. He never came with any agenda except finding a way to connect them with God's truth.

With radical honesty, there is no hidden agenda or desire to manipulate for an intended outcome. It's radical because it's genuinely humble and not self-seeking. Conversations marked by radical honesty never start with how the other person is wrong and how you're right.

Radical honesty comes from meekness and being truly authentic. It shares your humanity, your imperfections, and your limitations, along with your dreams and desires.

There is nothing more transformational than confessing when you see where you've been acting deceptively and living insincerely. When you are honest with those impacted by your deceit, you can begin to restore what wasn't working.

This is radical honesty. It doesn't need to explain or excuse the way things have been; rather, it owns every bit of the responsibility of getting the speck out of your eye and restoring this area with no desire to pass judgment and make others wrong.

## SHIFT IN FOCUS

Radical honesty isn't about looking good but sharing your humanity with those in your life. In light of this, looking at those areas where you saw some element of deceit, what would be the most authentic and genuine thing you could share? What actions would best restore this area of your life?

Pick a time to share what you've discovered through the work you've done. Powerfully connect with this person and genuinely share your inauthenticity, and reflect the love of Christ to them by restoring this area.

Remember, Jesus isn't about having people feel wrong or right, but seeking repentance and restoration. He wants you to live authentically to who you are and the life He has given you.

# DAY 19 • • • • • • • • • • • •
When Honesty Causes Conflict

*Repay no one evil for evil, but give thought to do what is honorable
in the sight of all. If possible, so far as it depends on you,
live peaceably with all.*
(Romans 12:17–18)

One of the reasons radical honesty can be so hard is because
you will also find conflict where there is integrity and honesty.
People are comfortable with being lied to, at least a little, especially if it's for the sake of stroking their ego or not calling out
their sin. So if you're going to be honest in love, you're also going
to have to deal with conflict in love.

This may *feel* horrible in the moment, and other people may
even make you feel like you've done something wrong, but this is
what a God-honoring lifestyle requires. Our feelings are not the
best indicator of truth when it comes to conflict. Conflict can feel
horrible yet still be good and produce godliness.

So what tools do we use when dealing with conflict in a
godly way?

+ **Use a gentle voice and say kind yet true words.** Don't
  go for low blows. If you feel yourself getting heated or
  losing control, ask for a break.

+ **Own your part, and ask for forgiveness.** None of us is
  without sin. Look long and hard for your part in causing
  the conflict and be humble about asking for forgiveness.

+ **Bring a mediator or unbiased party.** I think we often skip bringing in a mediator because it can make a conflict feel like a big deal, but often a mediator will *prevent* your conflict from turning into a big deal.

+ **Give it time.** Not all conflicts will be resolved in one conversation. As painful as it may be, keep taking the time to work on it (if both parties are willing) until there has been some form of reconciliation.

+ **Prepare.** Ask people to pray for you as you head into difficult situations. Spend time with God, searching for His will and letting Him guide your next steps. Read books like *Boundaries* by Henry Cloud and John Townsend, and *Pursuing Peace* by Robert D. Jones.

As you use these tools and humbly let God guide your conflicts, you'll have the clear conscience to know that you're living peaceably, *"so far as it depends on you."*

## SHIFT IN FOCUS

Take a moment to dissect why conflict feels so hard.

Are you afraid you'll lose a relationship? Do you feel ill prepared? Did you sin and don't want to own up to it?

# DAY 20 • • • • • • • • • • •

When Honesty Causes Loss

*But he said to me, "My grace is sufficient for you, for my power is made perfect in weakness." Therefore I will boast all the more gladly of my weaknesses, so that the power of Christ may rest upon me.* (2 Corinthians 12:9)

**D**ear Achiever, what are you afraid of losing? Deceit can often be a protective measure against loss, whether that be the loss of a relationship, loss of respect, loss of your job, loss of health—the list could go on and on. We lie not for the fun of it or because we're bad people, but because we are protecting ourselves against something.

In the Bible, Paul was someone who literally lost it all. He had wealth, esteem, power, and respect. But that all changed when he encountered God, and God changed his heart. Paul became the crazy Jesus guy who would live out his years preaching and teaching while people tried to kill him because of his beliefs. He was shipwrecked, imprisoned, separated from the people he loved, beaten, stoned, and ultimately killed for his faith.

But Paul clung to this:

*For I am sure that neither death nor life, nor angels nor rulers, nor things present nor things to come, nor powers, nor height nor depth, nor anything else in all creation, will be able to separate us from the love of God in Christ Jesus our Lord.* (Romans 8:38–39)

The good news of the gospel—a word that literally means *good news*—is that God loves us and wants us to spend eternity with Him.

> *I give them eternal life, and they will never perish, and no one will snatch them out of my hand.* (John 10:28)

This life on earth is temporary; whatever we lose when we follow God's commands is worth the loss, even if it feels painful at the time. If we want to live a life obedient to Christ, we make uncomfortable choices that may cause loss. Not because we are afraid of punishment, trading one fear for another, but because we are responding to the indescribable love of our Creator and believing He knows what's best for us.

---

## SHIFT IN FOCUS

As we wrap up these ten hard days on deceit, I want to leave you encouraged that nothing, not even your own sin, will separate you from Christ.

> *In him we have redemption through his blood, the forgiveness of our trespasses, according to the riches of his grace.*
> (Ephesians 1:7)

Past, present, and future sins are all covered by the blood of Jesus. You no longer have to live in shame over them. (See Romans 8:1.)

The life of a Christian is one of constant humbling, seeing our sin, failures, and weaknesses and using them as an opportunity to praise the God who died for us knowing the exact depths of our crooked hearts.

Don't let your sin being called out make you hide in shame; that's exactly what Satan wants. Your reflection of God is too loud and too powerful to have you both moving forward in action *and* living in humble repentance. Satan will try his hardest to stop your action or stop you from growing in humility.

Take a moment to thank God for revealing sin in your life and for giving you such a powerful purpose. Pray against Satan's scheme against you.

# 10 DAYS OF ENCOURAGEMENT
*Your Strength and How to Use It*

• • • • • • • • • • • **DAY 21**

*What Is Encouragement?*

*Therefore encourage one another and build one another up,*
*just as you are doing.*
(1 Thessalonians 5:11)

**G**od made us to need each other. We weren't meant to go through life without relationships, and encouragement is a huge part of that. Giving someone our support, confidence, or hope is one way we can help each other and bear each other's burdens. (See Galatians 6:2.)

We support someone when we remind them of their own talents, abilities, and the power of Christ in them. We can supply confidence to someone who is feeling apprehensive or hesitant on their own by giving them a pep talk. And we can help the people around us to hope when they're tempted to despair by reminding them of who their hope is in. When the specifics in our lives change, God's faithfulness does not.

As a Three, this is a huge gifting of yours. We see Threes all throughout culture who are adored because of how they encourage others. I've personally seen this gifting play out in the Threes in my own life. Tyler Zach, whose story you read at the beginning of this book, often sends a private message to encourage me. Jena Stagner, who wrote many of these devotionals, is a consistent cheerleader in my life. And my mom is a Three who can encourage my heart like no one else. Threes can use their gifts to be a blessing to others.

In fact, you may find yourself in a career where encouragement is a day-to-day activity, such as pastoring, teaching, or public speaking. But I've also seen Threes take almost any position and make encouragement part of their job description. It's just second nature to Achievers. And encouragement is a necessity in all fields.

Dear Three, this gifting of yours might feel so easy to you that you don't place much value on it. However, it is life-giving, both to those you encourage and to you as you see those around you grow under your words and actions.

## SHIFT IN FOCUS

When was the last time you were truly encouraged by someone?

Make a point to pick two people this week whom you will go out of your way to encourage. This practice will help you to be mindful of this gift in yourself, and it will bless the people you select.

Write the names of the people you pick as well as how you will encourage them, whether by text, in person, on the phone, sending a card, or some other means.

_____,

who I will encourage by

_____

_____,

who I will encourage by

_____

# DAY 22 • • • • • • • • • • •

*Designed to See Others' Potential*

*For we are his workmanship, created in Christ Jesus for good works, which God prepared beforehand, that we should walk in them.* (Ephesians 2:10)

Our chief want is someone who will inspire us
to be what we know we could be.
—Ralph Waldo Emerson

One of the things that makes you especially gifted in encouragement is your ability to see the potential in others. As an Enneagram Three, you are typically a mixture of being motivated by worth, future-focused, and success-oriented. All of these characteristics combine to help you spot potential from a mile away.

Some Threes might use this gift to spot their potential competition and tear them down, while others might use it to pick the most unsuspecting people for their team project. Still other Achievers use it to get ahead of the stock market. But most Threes use this ability to spot others' strengths and call that out. The latter is an act of encouragement in the most basic sense.

Do you find yourself people watching? Can you tell who the most successful or likable person in the room is? Do you have an intuition about the potential in kids or teenagers? Are you pained when the people around you waste their capabilities? This is all a part of your talent in spotting potential.

This gifting makes you a huge asset during the casting-vision season of entrepreneurship. It makes you a great interviewer, an inspirational speaker, and a motivating leader.

Encouraging is a way you use this talent no matter what your job field or season of life. Encouraging others toward their potential makes you instrumental in making the world a better place and making others' lives more fulfilling.

## SHIFT IN FOCUS

Who do you know who isn't living up to their full potential?

Write them a message or card, encouraging them in the giftings and potential you see in them. You don't have to tell them what to do with their life, or that they're wasting their potential. Instead, share what you see as their gifts, talents, and strengths, and let their imagination and encouraged heart do the rest.

# DAY 23 • • • • • • • • • • •

*A High Demand Job: The World Needs Encouragers*

*Peace I leave with you; my peace I give to you. Not as the world
give do I give to you. Let not your hearts be troubled,
neither let them be afraid.*
(John 14:27)

Encouragement lifts downfallen spirits, moves lazy feet to action, and turns anxiety into peace. Like water for a wilting plant, it is the substance by which we grow.

The truth is we all *need* encouragement, so in this way, you are an essential worker. This can feel draining, daunting even, but it is also a life-giving calling. In today's Scripture from the Gospel of John, we see why we are all starved for encouragement. It's not because our friends aren't sharing enough inspirational quotes on Facebook, or the people around us don't tell us how wonderful we are. We like those things, but they are not the encouragement we actually need.

John quotes Jesus as saying, *"Not as the world gives do I give to you."* The encouragement the world gives is fleeting and shallow; it doesn't water us down to our roots. The world's encouragement is like jelly beans given to sustain us while we are running a marathon when what we really need are water, carbs, and foods of substance. We end up parched and wondering if maybe we just need *more* jelly beans.

As an encourager in this parched world, you can choose to heap on the jelly beans, or you can offer not what comes from the world, but what comes from Christ.

Here's an example of worldly encouragement versus godly encouragement:

- Worldly encouragement: "You look so cute today!"

- Godly encouragement: "I can tell how much you love Jesus by how dedicated you are in your work."

- Worldly encouragement: "You're such a good mom!"

- Godly encouragement: "I admire the way you pour into your children, even on hard days. It shows that you truly believe children are a blessing."

- Worldly encouragement: "I love your house!"

- Godly encouragement: "Whenever we come to your house, I feel so welcome and taken care of. Thank you for blessing us with your gift of hospitality."

Your calling to encourage can be a life-giving one when you choose to give people godly encouragement that sustains their spirits.

---

## SHIFT IN FOCUS

What's an example of worldly encouragement you hear almost every day versus a word of encouragement that's stuck with you over time?

Take a moment to pray and thank God for letting you be a part of encouraging His people. If these words reflect your heart, please borrow them:

> Dear heavenly Father, I thank You for being the ultimate encourager and enabling me to share in a small part of what that looks like here on earth. Please empower me to be a godly encourager and to encourage others in the way that You see them. Send people into my life to encourage, and bring them to my mind often. Also, send people into my life to encourage me. Thank You for how You encourage my heart, Father. Amen.

• • • • • • • • • • • **DAY 24**

*Encouragement in the Bible*

> *Thus Joseph, who was also called by the apostles Barnabas*
> *(which means son of encouragement), a Levite, a native of Cyprus,*
> *sold a field that belonged to him and brought the money and*
> *laid it at the apostles' feet.*
> (Acts 4:36–37)

**B**arnabas is a relatively minor character in the Bible, mentioned only twenty-eight times, twenty-five of which are in the book of Acts.

Barnabas was a Christian leader and teacher in the days of Paul who vouched for Paul to other church officials after Paul's miraculous conversion.

> *And when he had come to Jerusalem, he attempted to join*
> *the disciples. And they were all afraid of him, for they did*
> *not believe that he was a disciple. But Barnabas took him*
> *and brought him to the apostles and declared to them how*
> *on the road he had seen the Lord, who spoke to him, and*
> *how at Damascus he had preached boldly in the name of*
> *Jesus. So he went in and out among them at Jerusalem,*
> *preaching boldly in the name of the Lord.* (Acts 9:26–28)

This encounter took place after Paul's escape from Damascus, when Jews had plotted to kill him. (See Acts 9:22–23.) So Barnabas's faith in Paul not only gave him a place among the apostles but probably saved his life. I imagine that this beginning is what led to a long relationship between Paul and Barnabas, as well as ministry life together. Paul refers to Barnabas several times in his letters.

One thing to note is that Barnabas was not his real name, but a nickname for this man named Joseph. We see this quite a bit in the Bible. Simon was called Peter, meaning "rock," and we are told that Thomas was called Didymus, or "the twin," which some scholars think is because he bore a striking resemblance to Jesus Himself.

Barnabas means "son of encouragement," which suggests that this man who came to Paul's defense was known so widely for his encouragement that it became his nickname.

We are not given specific examples of how Barnabas was encouraging in the Bible, but that doesn't mean that we can't be emboldened by his example. He was empowered by the same Holy Spirit you are, and with His help, you too can be known by your encouraging presence.

---

## SHIFT IN FOCUS

Do you think you're known for encouraging?

Paul might be a prominent character in the Bible, but the people who supported him and enabled him to keep going are just as important. Do you have a Barnabas in your life? Send them a text or card today to thank them for supporting you.

• • • • • • • • • • **DAY 25**

*Encouragement in History*

*I thank my God in all my remembrance of you.*
(Philippians 1:3)

History is a great place to look for encouragers. There are so many stories of mothers, siblings, bosses, spouses, friends, and others who changed the lives of those around them with their encouragement.

Here is just one of those stories.

Abraham Lincoln was born on February 12, 1809, to Thomas and Nancy Lincoln. They already had a daughter named Sarah; Abraham was their first son. He was awkward and gangly, even from the beginning, but very bright. His mother encouraged his sharp mind and love of reading. She also encouraged moral uprightness and honesty in her son.

Nancy Lincoln died when Abraham was only nine years old, but her impact has been felt by generations.

"All that I am, or hope to be, I owe to my angel mother," Abraham Lincoln once said.

A year after her death, Abraham's father remarried. Abraham's stepmother, the former Sarah Bush Johnston, is said to have brought life and comfort back into the family home. Their relationship was not instant, but Abraham and his stepmother would eventually create a strong bond. She recognized herself in him and fought for his right to pursue education. The support and encouragement Sarah Lincoln gave her stepson is one that cannot be rivalled. She adored him and believed in him, and he would call her "mother" for the remainder of his life, feeling her encouragement even from states away.

As we recognize the legacy of these two women, it is important that we also remember the Scripture for today. Encouragement is a fruit of the work of Christ in these people's lives. We do not owe any special gratitude to them for being "so encouraging," but we owe thanks to God, who empowered them to be figures of encouragement in others' lives. More importantly, their God is the same God who is working in your life today.

---

## SHIFT IN FOCUS

If you are a parent, do you see encouragement as a primary job in your life with your children?

How does this story from more than two hundred years ago encourage your heart today?

## • • • • • • • • • • • DAY 26

*Encouraging in the Church*

*Not neglecting to meet together, as is the habit of some,*
*but encouraging one another,*
*and all the more as you see the Day drawing near.*
(Hebrews 10:25)

Most of the verses pertaining to encouragement in the New Testament are speaking about encouragement within the church. Paul applauds churches whose members are encouraging one another and rebukes those churches that don't do likewise.

In this verse from Hebrews, there is an interesting connection between neglecting to meet together and not encouraging each other. Even in our digital age, it can be hard to think of others or specifically go out of our way to encourage others if we don't know what is happening in their lives. When we are involved with the church body, other people's problems, circumstances, and need for encouragement become more obvious. When we prioritize meeting, whether in a Sunday church service context or in smaller groups throughout the week, we are opening ourselves up to being poured out in encouragement toward our brothers and sisters in Christ.

Here are some practical ways we can encourage others in the church:

## PRIORITIZE SHOWING UP

If you don't go to a local church, try to find one, get in the habit of going every week you can, join a small group, and let God do the work in your life and the lives of others.

## SPEAK UP

Don't assume someone is getting encouraged by others in the church. If you see an area where you could encourage someone, do it!

## CHALLENGE YOURSELF

Challenge yourself to encourage at least two people on Sunday mornings, and three people throughout the week through a text, email, card, phone call, etc.

## GIVE YOURSELF GRACE

You won't be perfect at this, and you don't need to be. Take baby steps, and don't let missing weeks (or months) of church or not meeting your challenges discourage you.

---

## SHIFT IN FOCUS

Are there a couple of faces that come to mind when you think of encouraging people within your church?

Does encouraging people at church come naturally to you, or do you struggle here? Why do you think that is?

If you don't go to church, what is a step you could take today toward trying out a church in your area? Do you need to get recommendations from Facebook friends? Would you like a friend to go with you to try one out? Do you need to prioritize getting some counseling to heal from church hurt?

# DAY 27 • • • • • • • • • • •

*When Encouraging Means Others Don't See Your Needs*
*By Jena Stagner*

*And my God will supply every need of yours according*
*to his riches in glory in Christ Jesus.*
(Philippians 4:19)

*For whatever was written in former days was written for our*
*instruction, that through endurance and through the encouragement*
*of the Scriptures we might have hope.*
(Romans 15:4)

Speaking the good you see in those around you comes naturally to you as a Three, but this way of living isn't natural for everyone. You know the power words have on people and that having someone speak truth into your life would make a difference.

You may wish someone would come into your life and see you the same way you see others, providing the rich and valuable words of encouragement that would give you hope.

Living with this expectation unfulfilled can lead to resentment if not surrendered. Feelings of resentment could impact your gift of encouragement by causing you to take your eyes off the abundance you have and instead focus on your lack.

When you are present with an unmet need, the first best step is to surrender and trust your needs to Jesus—having faith that God will supply for your every need. Seeking sufficiency in God will always produce a beautiful result of endurance and encouragement.

Once you have surrendered and trusted God with your needs, there are two other steps of faith you can take:

1.  Look for a way to meet this need in a healthy way.

2.  Share your need with another Christian, asking for help in navigating this.

Since you can see others at their core, it is easy to feel that others fail to see who you authentically are and meet your needs.

Others do not have this same gifting of Threes, so you must share authentically about your life in order for others to know your needs—not just sharing the wins, accomplishments, and things that make you look good but also the hardships, trials, and struggles.

Sharing the real you in these areas helps others see ways that they can serve you. If people don't know, they can't act. Connect with people by sharing your needs and admit that you don't have it all together, because there is a good chance they think you do.

## SHIFT IN FOCUS

What do you need? Share this with God and surrender any feelings you're holding onto that might be leading to resentment. Repent of any pride that is giving others a wrong impression of your needs.

Who in your life could you share your needs with? Try telling this person that you don't need them to fix anything but that you trust them enough to share this with them, and this is an area you're looking to grow in.

You might be surprised what you hear as a response to your authentic sharing of yourself with them.

• • • • • • • • • • • **DAY 28**

*When Encouraging Isn't Natural*

*Do nothing from selfish ambition or conceit, but in humility count others more significant than yourselves. Let each of you look not only to his own interests, but also to the interests of others.*
(Philippians 2:3–4)

Dear Achiever, how often do you cringe as someone leads a meeting, casts vision, or fumbles through a live video feed that you could've done better? I've come to notice that the areas we are strongest in tend to bring us the most annoyance when they're lacking in others. For us, these things are easy, so it almost seems like they're *trying* to do them wrong.

This is one of the areas where I see Threes missing out on an opportunity to encourage. You might take someone's failure as a chance to bolster yourself or talk about them behind their back to others. But really, this is a moment for your encouragement to shine. No doubt, the person you're criticizing in your head already feels everything you're noticing, and what they could use is some encouragement. This definitely doesn't mean you need to lie, but pick one thing that is true, and applaud that.

This could sound as simple as, "I loved how you started with prayer!" or "You have a lot of wisdom" or "The closing point that you made was really good!"

Another situation where encouragement can be hard is when you know someone did really well, and it feels threatening. Maybe you have a friendly competition with a coworker, or your sibling is pursuing the same career field as you. It can be really hard to encourage someone when their success feels like it might take something away from you. But that's scarcity thinking! Living in an abundance mindset means that we can all succeed, and that doesn't steal anything away from you.

---

## SHIFT IN FOCUS

This week, make a point to notice when encouraging is hard for you. Prepare yourself for those situations by rehearsing quick and true encouragements you can send someone's way. Even if you forget to do it in person, don't let that stop you from sending a quick email or text. It will probably mean a lot more than you realize.

## • • • • • • • • • • • DAY 29

### When Encouraging Leaves You Empty
#### By Jena Stagner

*I appeal to you therefore, brothers, by the mercies of God,
to present your bodies as a living sacrifice, holy and acceptable
to God, which is your spiritual worship.*
(Romans 12:1)

**W**hen we surrender our life to Jesus, we say yes to presenting our bodies as a living sacrifice. When we feel empty and let the gospel fill us, this is evidence we are living like Christ, as Paul tells the church at Corinth: *"Be imitators of me, as I am of Christ"* (1 Corinthians 11:1).

As imitators, feeling empty without Christ is evidence of a faithful life. The breakdown happens when we swap our feelings for our identity. We then can go from feeling empty to living as if we *are* empty, which results in a very ineffective life for the gospel.

When you pour yourself out to encourage others and you feel empty at the end of the day, what do you tell yourself? If you say, "I'm so exhausted" or "I'm alone," you are speaking lies over your life.

Your identity isn't exhausted or alone. You are a child of God who happens to *feel* exhausted and alone. There is nothing you can do about your identity as a child of God, and there is so much you can do to change your state of being.

The first thing you can do is begin to speak the truth over this area of your life. Seek out Scripture and take actions to care for yourself if you feel exhausted or alone.

What do you need to do when you feel exhausted? Do you need to take a nap or read a book? What would restore you? Are you spending time in God's Word regularly? Are you getting a weekly Sabbath rest and living without deceit when it comes to your schedule and capacity?

What about feeling alone? Who do you know who you could call or meet up with for a cup of coffee? They could use the connection as much as you do. And if there are no actions you can take, hold onto the truth in Scripture that says we are never alone.

If we neglect these areas that God designed to fill up, we will pour from an empty cup. We want to live our lives as a sacrifice and to imitate Christ, but we must honor and steward our humanity that has many needs.

When you reach the end of yourself and you've done everything you can and you still feel empty, find encouragement in God's Word with verses like this one:

> *Likewise the Spirit helps us in our weakness. For we do not know what to pray for as we ought, but the Spirit himself intercedes for us with groanings too deep for words.*
>
> (Romans 8:26)

## SHIFT IN FOCUS

What identity statements do you see yourself saying lately? Keep a notepad next to you or on your phone today and see if you can catch yourself saying or thinking an identity statement such as, "I'm exhausted," "I'm tired," or "I'm alone." Write down anything that isn't in alignment with your identity in Christ. Reframe these statements as the feelings they are. For example, "I am a child of God who feels exhausted, tired, or alone." Whatever your list might be, write it out and keep it nearby.

Standing in the fullness of Christ, what actions can you take to care for the needs of your current state of being? Create a list of what you might do, pick something that would make a difference, and work to complete that.

# DAY 30 • • • • • • • • • • • •

*Encouraging to the Glory of Christ*

*May the God of endurance and encouragement grant you to live in such harmony with one another, in accord with Christ Jesus.*
(Romans 15:5)

**B**eing an encourager can be hard, tiring, and thankless work. However, your role as an encourager brings glory to God and is a way you reflect Him to the people around you.

In the verse for today, we see God referred to as the *"God of...encouragement."* Encouragement is in God's heart for His children, and when you encourage your brothers and sisters, you get to help remind them of God's heart for them.

The goal of encouragement is not that you would be thanked or praised for your goodness, but that God would be praised.

The other day, I was struggling with everything on my plate, feeling overwhelmed and purposeless, when an encouraging message popped up in my inbox unprompted. The person sending the message could not have known the state of my heart, but God did. And I am so grateful God used this message and this friend to encourage me. All I could do was thank God for His goodness and timing. This is how encouragement should make others feel. When we are obedient to the Holy Spirit's prompting, we get to be a part of bringing glory to Christ.

The *Westminster Shorter Catechism* states, "Man's chief end is to glorify God, and to enjoy him forever." It reflects

1 Corinthians 10:31, which reads, *"So, whether you eat or drink, or whatever you do, do all to the glory of God."*

When we are bringing glory to God, we are living out our purpose, no matter what our profession, season of life, or situation.

---

## SHIFT IN FOCUS

Think of the times you felt the most purposeful and connected to God.

In those times, were you bringing glory to Him?

Spend some time thanking God for your role in bringing glory to Him through encouraging others.

# 10 DAYS OF EXAMINING SUCCESS ORIENTATION
Help with a Common Pain Point

## DAY 31 • • • • • • • • • •
*Being Motivated by Worth*

*Do not be conformed to this world, but be transformed by the renewal of your mind, that by testing you may discern what is the will of God, what is good and acceptable and perfect.*
(Romans 12:2)

**A**s a Three, your main motivation is worth—to have self-worth or add worth or value to the world around you. All Threes want to prove to themselves and others that they add value to the world; this is in essence what makes you a type Three.

This unquenchable thirst for value or worth often leads Threes to shed their quirks, becoming more approachable to others in order to become likable, successful, or even valuable as they try to make an impact. Each Three's gauge of what success looks like will be different, but the drive to achieve whatever they view as success can be found in all Threes. This is why you might look very different from the other Threes in your life, or how type Threes are described in general.

Some Threes view their worth as being tied to their profession—they want to be the best and excel in their careers. Others want their garden to be the envy of the neighborhood. Still others will find success and worth in relationships.

Having a Two wing will usually make your success more relationship focused, while a Four wing will make you want to pursue unique things or be successful in a singular way.

In a Three's mind, success is equal to worth and value. The momentary high you gain from earning praise is difficult to beat, and when what you do determines your worth, you're often highly motivated. This is why Threes are often successful in their fields; they have to be, as their identity depends on it. This can look great from the outside, but when you give so much power to what others define as success or achievement, it can cause burnout, depression, and spiritual atrophy on the inside.

In the verse for today, we see that we are not to be conformed to the world and what it says success looks like; rather, we are to transform our thinking to what God thinks of us and His will for us.

Jesus was not a very successful or impressive man by worldly standards, and that certainly didn't matter. It's not that He couldn't have been powerful or wealthy; in fact, people were basically begging Him to become king, and Satan even tempted Him in the desert with power on earth. But Jesus's eyes were firmly fixed on His father, and the approval of man couldn't touch His identity as the Son of God.

---

## SHIFT IN FOCUS

As you consider this motivation for success and how it has impacted your life, whose approval would you say you're trying to gain?

How would your trajectory change if you didn't have to do anything to have worth?

• • • • • • • • • • • **DAY 32**

*Inherent Worth*

*For you formed my inward parts; you knitted me together in my mother's womb. I praise you, for I am fearfully and wonderfully made. Wonderful are your works; my soul knows it very well.*
(Psalm 139:13–14)

**T**wos, Threes, and Fours in the heart triad all share the mistaken belief that they lack inherent worth. Because this isn't a term we use every day, let's quickly define *inherent*. This word means existing in something as a permanent or essential space. Basically, we struggle to believe our worth is permanent or that we are essential.

Not believing in our inherent worth means that we feel like we need to *do something* in order to have worth. Twos need to be of use or helpful, Threes need to be successful or productive, and Fours need to add something new or unique to the world around them. But the truth is that none of us have to *do anything* to have worth and value—we are not the ones who give ourselves value.

Your worth is inherent because God gave it to you. He formed you in your mother's womb and numbered every one of your days. He gave you worth and value because He made you. You have a soul, you reflect your God, and you were purposefully, wonderfully, and exceptionally made.

But He didn't just form you and leave you. God loved you so dearly that He sent Jesus to pay the ultimate price for you, even when you were undeserving. Romans 5:8 says: *"But God shows his love for us in that while we were still sinners, Christ died for us."* This is the good news of the gospel and the assurance of the freedom in which we get to live in Christ. If you need proof of God's love for you, look to the cross.

---

## SHIFT IN FOCUS

*Nothing you have done or will ever do will diminish or add to the worth and value you had the moment you were conceived.*

Breathe deeply…and then read that sentence again.

Now read that sentence aloud, but replace "you" with "I."

There is so much freedom and grace in that fact, isn't there?

## • • • • • • • • • • • DAY 33

### What Satan Tells You About Your Worth

*Be sober-minded; be watchful. Your adversary the devil prowls*
*around like a roaring lion, seeking someone to devour.*
(1 Peter 5:8)

We have talked about how you reflect God to the rest of the world—but that honor comes at a price. We have an enemy because our Savior has an enemy. Satan's goal is to win your soul, but if he can't have your eternity, he will try to steal your joy, peace, and effectiveness here on earth.

Our doubts about our worth and purpose can be tied back to carefully crafted lies from Satan, the father of lies. The devil *"does not stand in the truth, because there is no truth in him. When he lies, he speaks out of his own character, for he is a liar and the father of lies"* (John 8:44).

Satan tells you:

+ *You'll never be worth anything.*

+ *Why do you even try?*

+ *See, you can never do anything right.*

+ *What would they think of you if they really knew who you were?*

+ *Why did you just say that? They're going to think you're so stupid.*

These are all whispers from your enemy, who wants you to doubt what God created you to be. He wants you to be paralyzed, to stop trying. And the shame he lays on your heart is as thick as tar.

It's important to be aware that this is a spiritual battle because many of us assume these thoughts come from us. We call them self-doubt, low self-confidence, or self-pity. But these are often an attack from the father of lies. We view and react to these moments very differently when we understand that they're leveled against us instead of self-inflicted.

So what can we do when we hear these lies? We can rebuke them—literally tell Satan to eat dirt, tell him he's not welcome in our ears and we won't listen to him. We have authority here; we are not under Satan's thumb, and by the power of Jesus Christ, if we tell him to beat it in our Savior's name, he has to listen to us. (See Luke 10:19.)

If we are going to take on the lies of Satan, we also need to be students of the truth. It's very difficult to rebuke his lies if we are not immersed in God's Word. If we are hearing Satan's lies every day, then we need to read our Bible every day and hear from the Holy Spirit instead.

## SHIFT IN FOCUS

Read Ephesians 6:11–13.

What lies are you most tempted to believe about yourself?

What does God say that rebukes those specific lies?

• • • • • • • • • • • **DAY 34**

*Chasing Affirmation*

*Every athlete exercises self-control in all things. They do it to receive a perishable wreath, but we an imperishable. So I do not run aimlessly; I do not box as one beating the air.*
(1 Corinthians 9:25–26)

Praise, affirmation, and applause are addictive. Many of us spend a good bit of our time seeking ways to be affirmed and appreciated by others. We see people we think have achieved a life where they're confident, loved, and deeply adored by others, and we envision what their life must be like. We can't imagine them having the doubts we struggle with.

The problem is, we tend to only feel as good as our last accomplishment. That praise you received in high school, or even last week, loses its sparkle pretty quickly. It won't keep you going; you'll need to hear it more than just once, and big success needs to be followed up with even bigger success. This is one of the reasons we are so tired: we are chasing the wind. Man's praise is perishable. Even accomplishment doesn't feel as satisfying as we think it will. If we become famous, it won't be enough, and no amount of money can really make us happy. I think deep down we know this, but it doesn't keep us from wanting to prove those suspicions to ourselves.

Sometimes there is nothing scarier than reaching your biggest goals. The question, "What's next?" weighs heavily on us.

And now people are watching. We think, *What if this is it? What if this is as good as I'll ever be?* This thought can be terrifying.

In 1 Corinthians 9, we see Paul comparing life to a race. As Christians, we need to keep ourselves in check, exercising self-control and staying focused on our goal to glorify God and enjoy Him forever. Lasting peace, confidence, hope, and joy are found in this imperishable mission.

Our hope is not found in success, praise, or affirmation. It is not found in achieving, earning fame, or even receiving love from those we want it from the most. No. Our security, worth, and hope are in Christ.

## SHIFT IN FOCUS

Spend some time checking your heart with God.

Are you motivated more by man's praise than by God's glory?

Do you often feel frustrated by the fleeting nature of praise?

How would your life change if you made it your goal to glorify God instead of seeking praise, success, or love for yourself?

Bring these questions to God and pray that He will soften your heart and show you how He wants you to respond.

• • • • • • • • • • • **DAY 35**

Too Busy to Stop

*Come to me, all who labor and are heavy laden, and I will give you*
*rest. Take my yoke upon you, and learn from me, for I am gentle*
*and lowly in heart, and you will find rest for your souls. For my yoke*
*is easy, and my burden is light.*
(Matthew 11:28–30)

We all hit a wall eventually, but as a Three, you might run a little longer than the rest of us. Along with Sevens and Eights, you have much more energy at your disposal than many others. This is fortunate because being motivated by worth can mean your life looks like a perpetual hamster wheel. Once you've accomplished one thing, you're on to the next without so much as batting an eyelash. You thrive off productivity, future plans, and constantly accomplishing bigger and better things. This can make things like rest, silence, or vacation feel very hard to prioritize. The high of accomplishment is just too satisfying to set aside.

However, I've talked to Threes who are struggling with chronic fatigue; perhaps they are in the midst of chemo treatments, on bed rest, struggling with anemia, or raising very young children. These Threes find themselves forced to slow down in a way that's not only hard physically, but also causes them to struggle with their identity and worth. They think, *Who am I if I don't have the energy to run life at the pace that makes me feel valuable? Who am I with an empty calendar? Who am I when I'm the one needing help?* And they may not have an answer.

Unfortunately, there are too many Threes in the world who don't rest adequately and are *forced* to rest by some kind of stress-related illness, all because they don't know who they are if they're not busy achieving their next goal.

Thankfully we know that no matter our state of busyness, or whether we're productive or not, our worth does not fluctuate in Christ. We can lose all of our ability to be productive, impressive, or busy and not lose an iota of value in the sight of God. This is one of the reasons why God calls us to rest, not only in His commandments about Sabbath but also in what Jesus says in today's verse from Matthew. He will give us rest when we come to Him.

---

## SHIFT IN FOCUS

Take a moment to look up stress-related illnesses and how stress manifests in your body.

Write down any symptoms with which you're prone to struggle. Use these as a red-flag warning that you need to rest.

What do you struggle to prioritize most? For instance, it could be sleeping, drinking water, eating healthily, or taking a vacation.

What would going to God with this area of your life look like?

What does God's Word say about this particular topic you struggle with?

• • • • • • • • • • • **DAY 36**

*What If You Fail?*
*By Jena Stagner*

*For you know that the testing of your faith produces steadfastness.*
(James 1:3)

As a Three, you most likely aren't afraid to take action—but you fear failure. Failure presents a different story. Fear of failure can lurk in the shadows of your dreams, causing you to manipulate what you are doing or who you are being to avoid failure at all costs.

But what if failure didn't exist? What if failure was also success?

We may think we're playing it safe and taking wise actions to avoid failure, but when we avoid taking action, we avoid obedience to God. This stops us from experiencing the goodness He desires in our lives.

God is calling us to take action, and that means we will fall short. We are humans, and this is part of our life of faith. But when we fall short, we learn and we move on.

While God does not test us like a schoolteacher, He does test us daily—not to point out our failures or lack, but to produce steadfastness and grow our faith.

God is not judging us against perfection when it comes to our faithful actions. Our perfection comes by believing in the death, burial, and resurrection of Jesus. This gives us space to try and risk failure, knowing there is no failure in Christ.

While God doesn't desire us to sin, He does desire us to try, which means there are times when we won't succeed. But failure in Christ is different from the world's standard of failure. Our failure is not a failure of identity but action. We did not take the action that produced the intended result, so we get up and try again.

As it says in Proverbs 24:16, "*For the righteous falls seven times and rises again, but the wicked stumble in times of calamity.*"

When our identity is in Christ, we are free to fall, which also means we are free to fail. Because for the Christian, failure is a success because His power "*is made perfect in weakness*" (2 Corinthians 12:9).

It doesn't mean you get to take foolish actions and not experience consequences. But for the righteous, you can take a wrong step and get back up again.

Surrendering to Christ and trusting Him to lead the way offers us the space to learn from the misstep and try again. The foolish actions of the wicked will not produce the same result.

God desires us to take steps of faith, filled up with His love. When there is no fear, God's love is then driving us. God tests you to help you grow, and He uses every faithful step to produce good fruit in you.

## SHIFT IN FOCUS

Take time today to journal about your fear of failure. Does this fear stop you from taking action? Repent and see what action God is calling you to choose today. What faithful step would you take if you couldn't fail? Identify a few areas of life you've been struggling to take action in and ask God to lead you while you brainstorm all you would do if you couldn't fail.

Dream big. God gave you your drive and ambition to give Him glory. You grow when you act, so take action with blessed assurance. Know that you may fall, but when you do, God will restore your steps and produce faith and steadfastness in you.

# DAY 37 • • • • • • • • • • •

What If Your Success Is Taken Away?
By Jena Stagner

*For by grace you have been saved through faith.*
*And this is not your own doing; it is the gift of God,*
*not a result of works, so that no one may boast.*
(Ephesians 2:8–9)

*See what kind of love the Father has given to us,*
*that we should be called children of God; and so we are.*
*The reason why the world does not know us is that it did not know*
*him. Beloved, we are God's children now, and what we will be has*
*not yet appeared; but we know that when he appears we*
*shall be like him, because we shall see him as he is.*
(1 John 3:1–2)

As an Achiever, you often find your mind flooded with "what if" questions when uncertainty strikes. The bigger the step or maybe even the leap you're taking, the greater the temptation to assess from a place not of wisdom but of fear.

You're gifted at considering so many variables regarding each step you take, assessing based on past knowledge, future anticipation, and the facts at hand at that moment. This processing, when done from surrender, can produce beautiful results. When done from fear, it can rob you of what God has for you in this place.

When you are operating from fear of man, your identity becomes what your actions are, leading you to identify as that which you can or can't accomplish. When you begin to identify with what you do or the success or failure you've experienced and not who you are in Christ, you can start to walk into dangerous territory.

You can become devastated and derailed in your ambition as you shift from surrender and obedience to control as you seek identity in something other than God.

When who you are departs from who God says you are, you will fail—and this is God's grace to us. When the things of this world fail us, we are forced to fall to our knees and seek restoration, getting us back on solid ground.

The success we are to live for cannot be taken from us. Our works are not what qualify us for the life Christ gives us. While our ambition moves us, if we find our identity in our worldly success alone, we are left with nothing if we lose it.

It is by God's grace that He gives us an unshakable identity so we can have unshakable faith, unable to be moved if we fail or lose our abilities.

---

## SHIFT IN FOCUS

What are you really great at? Where have you found success?

Do you identify with these accomplishments more than you identify with being a child of God?

Spend some time surrendering these gifts God has given to you. Honor Him for the work He has done in your life in leading you to where those accomplishments were possible.

Also, spend some time in prayer connecting with how truly loved you are regardless of anything you accomplish today. Nothing you do will change the love God has for you today. Thank Him for fully loving you for your identity and not your actions.

• • • • • • • • • • • **DAY 38**

## What If Someone Doesn't See You As Successful?

*Stop regarding man in whose nostrils is breath,*
*for of what account is he?*
(Isaiah 2:22)

Growing up, I received very different messages about college from my parents and grandparents. My grandparents were pro-college no matter what, while my parents were only in favor of college for careers in which it was absolutely required, such as becoming a doctor. In the years leading up to my college decisions, I felt confused and hesitant; I had to choose who to make happy and who to disappoint. I chose the vo-tech route and am currently a stay-at-home-mom with a career as an Enneagram coach. My grandparents are still disappointed I didn't attend college.

Maybe you have a similar story, but I think we live through these kinds of choices to some degree every day. *Who do I please and who do I disappoint?*

The Bible is clear that if the choice is between God's law and pleasing man, we must choose to obey God every time, no question. But often these choices are much more subtle. Your coworker is vegan, and if you bring a turkey sandwich to work, he gives you a disgusted look. Your cousin doesn't believe you should buy from Amazon, Target, or any big-box chain, and every year it's stressful to buy a Christmas gift for her. Your dad thinks your kids should be involved in more sports and brings it up every chance he gets. And Grandma gives you a piece of her mind if you dress your darling baby girl in any color other than pink. The examples could go on and on.

Trying to impress others and trying to be seen as great, successful, or even good in everyone's eyes is not a goal we can accomplish. And although we know this, it often doesn't stop us from trying. The times we do disappoint people still weigh heavily on us.

In Galatians 5:1, Paul writes, *"For freedom Christ has set us free; stand firm therefore, and do not submit again to a yoke of slavery."*

Jesus died so we could live in freedom—freedom from the rule of Satan but also freedom from needing to please mankind. When we make pleasing man our goal or put too much power in the opinion of those around us, we are submitting ourselves to a kind of slavery.

---

## SHIFT IN FOCUS

What opinions of man (that are not also laws of God) are uncomfortable for you?

What beliefs, pressures, and ideals of others do you carry with you that are unnecessary?

## • • • • • • • • • • • **DAY 39**

*Humility and How Failure Can Be a Blessing*
*By Jena Stagner*

> *For I have come down from heaven,*
> *not to do my own will but the will of him who sent me.*
> (John 6:38)

> *Every branch in me that does not bear fruit he takes away,*
> *and every branch that does bear fruit he prunes,*
> *that it may bear more fruit.*
> (John 15:2)

The life of Jesus reflects humility and shows how failure can be a blessing on the grandest scale. He lived only for the Father's will; by the world's standards, He failed, but God's will does not consider human measures of failure or success.

> *For my thoughts are not your thoughts, neither are your*
> *ways my ways, declares the LORD. For as the heavens are*
> *higher than the earth, so are my ways higher than your ways*
> *and my thoughts than your thoughts.* (Isaiah 55:8–9)

Humility can be hard to understand. Some believe it's playing small and staying quiet, but regardless of your understanding, *trying* to be humble can leave you self-consumed.

Timothy Keller says a helpful way to define humility is self-forgetfulness. The concern for humility goes away when you are living as a child of God focused on the Father's will. There isn't space to focus on self when you live in a state of self-forgetfulness.

When you take action without focusing on your identity, you are free to be your authentic self. There is no concern about falling or failing because you are living to please God, not man.

Living in fear of failure or avoiding hard things is not living for the will of the Father and forgetting self. John writes that those who bear fruit will be pruned. What may feel like failure is necessary to produce more fruit. There is no way to avoid the hard things of faith when you are not going your own way.

It may be challenging, and you may feel fear or anxiety. But in those moments, press into Jesus. Remember that the Father tends to His children so that they produce more fruit, bringing abundant blessing.

---

## SHIFT IN FOCUS

Do you know the will of the Father for your life? What action is the Holy Spirit calling you to take in faith at this moment?

Take a moment to be still and listen for His prompting. Maybe He's placed it on your heart to call a friend and pray over them. You are gifted as an Achiever to move forward and make things happen in Jesus's name.

As you share your gift for encouragement with others, strive to live from a place of self-forgetfulness, not concerned about your worldly identity or how your actions impact you. Instead, feel the joy of bearing fruit for God's kingdom.

## • • • • • • • • • • • DAY 40

*Humility and Your Identity in Christ*

> *He has told you, O man, what is good; and what does the* Lord
> *require of you but to do justice, and to love kindness,*
> *and to walk humbly with your God?*
> (Micah 6:8)

Humility is not being full of our own self-importance; it's not taking offense or defending ourselves in the face of rebuke or correction. Humility is knowing we have a lot of growth left to do.

Scripture calls us to walk humbly with our God, remembering that we are followers of Him along with our brothers and sisters in Christ. We are not the designers, orchestrators, or the ones in control of our life; God is.

None of us enjoy being around someone with delusions of grandeur who thinks they're more important than everyone else, but often we don't even realize *we* are that person until others won't put up with us anymore. God, in His kindness, will let us fail; He will let relationships break, and He will bring us to our knees one way or another.

In my study of the Enneagram, I have learned that there is a lesson Threes need to learn but can't be taught, and that's humility. When Threes experience a big failure in their lives, the result of that failure is growth and humility. Thus, failure can be a gift. And we learn that there is no mistake too big that God can't redeem it.

Walking in humbleness means we realize our worth is in what Christ has done for us, not in our business, our success, or how much people approve of us. This is the mark of a truly healthy Three. It might not ever feel natural, but God, in His goodness and by His Spirit, can make this change in you.

---

## SHIFT IN FOCUS

Take a moment to pray for a tender heart toward a conviction in this area. If these words reflect your heart, please borrow them:

> Dear heavenly Father, I admit that I am prone toward pride and wanting to accomplish everything in my own strength. I know humility is Your heart for me, and I want to bring glory to You by growing in this area. Please keep me tender toward conviction, as the Holy Spirit points out the areas of my life where I am struggling to be humble. I want to think rightly about my worth. Please help me in this area. Amen.

# 10 DAYS OF HANDLING SLOTH

*Going to Nine in Stress*

• • • • • • • • • • • **DAY 41**

*Seasons of Life*

*For everything there is a season, and a time for every matter under heaven: a time to be born, and a time to die; a time to plant, and a time to pluck up what is planted; a time to kill, and a time to heal; a time to break down, and a time to build up; a time to weep, and a time to laugh; a time to mourn, and a time to dance; a time to cast away stones, and a time to gather stones together; a time to embrace, and a time to refrain from embracing; a time to seek, and a time to lose; a time to keep, and a time to cast away; a time to tear, and a time to sew; a time to keep silence, and a time to speak; a time to love, and a time to hate; a time for war, and a time for peace.*

(Ecclesiastes 3:1–8)

In the whirlwind of life, expectations, and demands, it can be hard to think of ourselves as living seasonally. We live on an earth with winter, spring, summer, and fall, and we observe and celebrate the earth and its seasons, but we rarely give ourselves permission to change and transform. Instead, we expect all or nothing. Either I am...or I am not. There is *right now*, and anything worth doing is worth doing *today*. This is especially true in the hustle of America.

Of course, as we look at our own life, seasons are evident. There was that really hard year of illness, there were years of singleness, there were those amazing three months of falling in love, there were years with little kids, there were years of learning—everything in its own season.

We have a lot to learn from the way God created the earth with its seasons. In these verses from Ecclesiastes, Solomon notes there is a season for everything, and we can see that he's talking about us, not just the earth. The wisest king who ever lived says that for every bad or hard season we experience, there is a season of rest and good to come.

---

## SHIFT IN FOCUS

During the next nine days, we will go into detail about what a season of growth looks like for you as a Three.

As you look at your own life today, what season are you in? Read Ecclesiastes 3:1–8 again and pick one or two verbs that represent the season you're currently in.

Are you mourning, or celebrating?

Are you transitioning, or resting?

Are you uprooting, or planting?

If you're in a more hopeful, joyful, and restful season, it may be time to press into growth and celebrate the growth you can see in yourself. If you're in a season of difficulty, transition, and survival, it will be helpful for you to see this time as just a season, and see the hope on the horizon. You may even see some ways that you're growing even in stress and adversity.

Celebrate those wins!

# DAY 42 • • • • • • • • • • •

## What Is a Season of Stress?

*Blessed is the man who remains steadfast under trial,*
*for when he has stood the test he will receive the crown of life,*
*which God has promised to those who love him.*
(James 1:12)

In light of talking about seasons, I think we all know that there are seasons of stress we walk through. Some are lighter than others, but all bring the anxiety and feeling of just trying to survive that's familiar to us all.

When we talk about stress using Enneagram verbiage, we aren't talking about being late for work or losing your keys. We all get frustrated and irritable in those circumstances. No, when the Enneagram refers to stress, it means seasonal stress—you just lost your job, you're transitioning, your loved one just passed, and other harsh and trying circumstances. In those times, you're often in survival mode for months or years. This is the season of stress we are talking about.

During periods of seasonal stress, Threes will start to exhibit the unhealthy behaviors of Nines. You may lose energy and focus. All of a sudden, you're procrastinating and wasting time. Instead of relaxing, you may be numbing—tuning out your thoughts, your emotions, and the rest of the world. All of this is a cry for help.

These behaviors should serve as a stoplight for you to ask yourself a few questions:

- What is stressing me out right now?

- Am I currently in a season of stress?

- If I could look back on "me in stress" in another season, how would I be kinder to myself?

- Where should I be resting or giving myself more grace during this season?

Seasons of stress are nothing to be ashamed of. If anything, they cause us to cling to God in a really precious way and become highly aware of our need for Him.

---

## SHIFT IN FOCUS

Take a couple of moments to reflect on the season you're in right now. Is this a season of growth for you or a season of stress?

If it's a season of stress, take a deep breath, be kind to your battered heart, and cling to the Lord.

Steadfastness under trial is honoring to God, but that doesn't mean we should pretend there is no trial.

# DAY 43 • • • • • • • • • • •

*How Do I "Go To" Nine?*

*And he said, "My presence will go with you,
and I will give you rest."*
(Exodus 33:14)

As a Three, you should be able to look back at your life and see a pattern of Nine-ish behaviors during seasons of stress. You don't *become* a Nine by any means, but you do use their negative behaviors to cope with the stress you feel.

As you feel the toll of a season of stress, you gain coping skills to help yourself rest and not *feel* everything that's going on during this time. However, the coping skills you gain from going to Nine provide numbing instead of actual rest. You may be tempted to shut down and look for rest in mind-numbing behaviors such as eating, shopping, watching TV, and scrolling through social media for hours. This does help you to stop pouring energy out of your low reserve but does very little to fill you back up. So you end up stuck in stress and eventually leave this season less than proud of your stress behaviors.

What we really want is true rest that only God can provide as we trust Him to handle what's weighing us down. Going on a walk, reading our Bible, or investing in the things that truly fill us up are hard things to choose in stress—especially when the couch, a tub of ice cream, and Netflix are beckoning. Our culture champions our stress behaviors as self-care, which only helps to justify the temptation.

In reality, when you reach for the things that are most tempting in stress, you aren't solving anything, and you're not resting. You're numbing. You know that none of these things will truly help you in the long run, and they won't change whatever you're stressed about, but for an hour or two, you may not have to feel what's stressing you out—and that feels worth it in the moment.

Truly resting in Christ doesn't sound appealing because God won't let us become numb to the things we don't want to do; He calls us to faithfulness—to the better portion.

---

## SHIFT IN FOCUS

When you learn about your stress behaviors, you have more power to notice them when they pop up so you can ask yourself some pointed questions:

+ What am I stressed about?

+ Do I have an action step that I am avoiding?

+ What truly brings me rest?

Use the times you're tempted toward numbing as a sign to check in with yourself and God. During a time when you're not stressed, write a list of things that make you feel truly rested, and keep it on hand for times when you're tempted to choose the easier option.

# DAY 44 • • • • • • • • • • •

The Worst of Type Nine

*Go to the ant, O sluggard; consider her ways, and be wise. Without having any chief, officer, or ruler, she prepares her bread in summer and gathers her food in harvest. How long will you lie there, O sluggard? When will you arise from your sleep? A little sleep, a little slumber, a little folding of the hands to rest, and poverty will come upon you like a robber, and want like an armed man.*
(Proverbs 6:6–11)

**K**nown as the Peacemaker, the Enneagram Nine is truly moti-vated by peace and harmony. Healthy Nines are bold, decisive, and confident enough in themselves and their relationships to engage in healthy disagreements without feeling paralyzing fear. Trusting themselves and others, they no longer feel like they need to *go along* to *get along*, but focus on the long-term goals instead of just momentary peace in their relationships. Feeling self-aware and fulfilled, healthy Nines can put routines in their life to make sure they stay on task and do what is important.

Average, slightly unhealthy Nines will often say "yes" before realizing they don't actually mean it; they experience clouded judgment when they can sense what the other person wants. Since they avoid conflict at all costs, it's easy for other Enneagram types to boss these Nines around. Of course, they resent this and become quietly obstinate when they feel pushed.

Nines have a unique ability to merge with others, feeling what that person feels, giving them the empathy they need, and sometimes adopting their pain like it's a stray cat. An average Nine will view merging as how they care for others, without counting the cost to themselves personally. An unhealthy Nine will become detached and repressed, not wanting to be affected by life. The suppressed anger they've always had will now appear more often, causing others to become uneasy around the Nine. These Nines will be unpredictable, neglectful, and numb, making them dangerous to themselves and others.

It may feel a bit funny to be talking so much about Nines in a devotional meant for Threes, but because you go to Nine in stress, I want you to have a comprehensive look at what this type looks like. I can give you a list of behaviors that could be possible for you as you move to Nine in stress, but I could never think of all the practical ways this could play out for you.

So as you feel stressed, look at what being unaffected by life looks like for you. Have you experienced a version of merging during seasons of stress? This is a little different than projecting what you want others to see.

---

## SHIFT IN FOCUS

Do you have any Nines in your life? What do you see as their strengths and weaknesses?

It can be normal to feel especially irritated by the flaws we see in others that are true of ourselves as well. This shines a spotlight on something in us that we'd rather not see. When you're tempted to feel this way, ask yourself, "How is this irritating behavior true about me too? When do I do this?"

# DAY 45 • • • • • • • • • •

How Sloth Is Trying to Help

*Have you not known? Have you not heard? The LORD is the*
*everlasting God, the Creator of the ends of the earth. He does*
*not faint or grow weary; his understanding is unsearchable. He*
*gives power to the faint, and to him who has no might he increases*
*strength. Even youths shall faint and be weary, and young men shall*
*fall exhausted; but they who wait for the LORD shall renew their*
*strength; they shall mount up with wings like eagles; they shall run*
*and not be weary; they shall walk and not faint.*
(Isaiah 40:28–31)

The act of rest is built into the very fabric of our world. Even
before the fall of man and sin entering the world, God rested
on the seventh day as an example to us. (See Genesis 2:3.) As
we read in today's verses from Isaiah, God never grows weary—
but we do. So this example and later commandment to practice
Sabbath rest was for our good.

Rest can be hard for you as a Three because of your motivation of worth and the constant feeling that you need to be
productive. You may even trick yourself into believing you can
handle a faster and busier life than most with the help of coffee,
medication, and adrenaline.

But the realities of our body and mind's need for rest never
go away, and when you're stressed, your true fragility isn't as
armored as it normally is. Your need for rest is apparent and

demanding, but you might not be practiced in true rest—so sloth is here to help.

Sloth, when talked about as sin, is thought of as the avoidance of spiritual or physical activity rather than actual laziness. So, may I propose to you that instead of defining sloth as laziness, you think of it as numbing?

You can be very active physically and be using that activity to numb yourself to a conflict, a conviction, or even a task that really needs to be done. That's sloth. On the other hand, numbing can also look like sleeping or eating in excess, binge-watching TV, surfing the Internet—anything to avoid engaging in the present. This is also sloth.

I think sloth looks less like a whisper and more like the open arms of a hug. It says:

+ Come to me; you don't need to be here.

+ Escape in me. I have what will comfort you.

+ This is too much, isn't it? Taking this pill, signing up for one more class, watching that whole season on Netflix—those things will help you.

Sloth promises a lot that it can't actually deliver. We see in Scripture that our rest and strength come from the Lord. When we aren't engaging with our own soul by numbing, much less our Creator, we won't be accessing the true rest that God has for us.

Sloth may have good intentions, but it is a poor substitute for God's goodness when we humbly come to Him in our need.

## SHIFT IN FOCUS

Is this a new way of thinking about sloth for you?

As you process what going to God for rest means for you, try to think back to times when you felt the most whole and connected to God. What habits or activities were present in your life during those times?

• • • • • • • • • • • **DAY 46**

*The Temptation of Avoidance*
*By Alison Bradley*

*Let those who suffer according to God's will entrust their souls*
*to a faithful Creator while doing good.*
(1 Peter 4:19)

**D**ear Achiever, your strength of taking action can feel so challenging when there's no clear path forward. A stressful situation or season can make you feel like you're stuck. You long for a way to handle the hard things in your life, but when none is readily available, sloth offers the temptation of avoidance.

When things are hard, it is just so tempting to want to evade those things causing you stress. Perhaps, in order to deal with your stress, you avoid thinking about the difficulty at hand or push aside the grief that is bubbling to the surface. This is another way sloth might appear in your life, inviting you to avoid the painful aspects of your experience. Avoidance can feel like the answer in the moment. It promises you that your problem will go away if you don't think about it. It promises that if you don't give those unwanted emotions space, they'll just disappear.

But as I'm sure your head knows, even if your heart doesn't quite believe it at times, avoidance isn't the answer. Difficult things don't vanish just because you aren't looking at them or giving them attention. This is true not just for physical issues, but for emotional ones as well. Your disappointment at something not working out or your anger at an injustice done to someone you love doesn't just disappear because you are avoiding it. It may feel like that for a time, but the truth is that it is still there.

How do you create space for your stress? What does it mean for you to believe the truth that avoidance doesn't bring you the peace you crave?

I think it might be helpful to reframe your stress as suffering. How would it change things to think of your difficulties in this way? I know for my own heart, stress feels like something I should be able to manage myself. I try to avoid painful things and chase comfort in an attempt to handle my problems. But suffering feels different. Calling my stress *suffering* helps me believe the truth that I am in need of the Lord's help to show up here. I'm not facing this alone.

---

## SHIFT IN FOCUS

Spend a few minutes reading 1 Peter 4:12–19, paying special attention to the way Peter reminds us not to be surprised by suffering and invites us to entrust ourselves to the Lord. When you're finished reading this Scripture, pause and respond to what you've read. How might the Lord be inviting you to entrust yourself to Him today?

• • • • • • • • • • • **DAY 47**

*The Temptation to Numb*
*By Alison Bradley*

> *For thus said the Lord GOD, the Holy One of Israel,*
> *"In returning and rest you shall be saved; in quietness and in trust*
> *shall be your strength." But you were unwilling, and you said,*
> *"No! We will flee upon horses."*
> (Isaiah 30:15–16)

In a stressful season, our reserves are low and our energy wanes. This isn't a comfortable place to be in. While the specifics of our stress may be different from what the Israelites faced, I find my own temptation to numb in today's verses contrasted with the invitation from the Lord. I'm guessing you will too.

The Lord invites us to do what is counterintuitive when something is wrong.

*Rest. Return to Him. Be quiet. Trust.*

Notice our own tendency mirrored in the Israelites' response: to run away. Sin has altered our hearts so that instead of running *to* the Lord, our first instinct is to run away from Him. One of the ways we most often run away is through numbing.

Pause for a moment to consider how you are most often tempted to run away from what feels hard. Do you turn to your phone? Do you binge watch a show? Where do you see yourself tempted to run away from your unwanted emotions? Take a moment with the Lord to name that temptation. What do you want to tell Him about it?

Isaiah tells us that we run away because we are unwilling to allow the Lord to be our help. Running away from what is stressful or difficult in our life makes us think we're still in control, but it doesn't bring the relief and strength for which our hearts long. Let's look at the active way we can participate in our stress instead of running away and numbing. The Lord lovingly invites us into these things because He knows they will meet the true desires of our hearts.

## REST

Unlike numbing, where we are dimming our senses and ability to feel, true rest offers refreshment and calm. On the other side of rest, we feel a little more like our true selves. We have been cared for. We are actively choosing to trust that the Lord is working even if we are not.

## RETURNING TO HIM

We don't ignore our problems. Instead we bring them to the Lord. Sometimes I imagine myself handing Him the things that trouble me, placing them into His hands. This action is the opposite of numbing, as I'm acknowledging that the One who can best handle the issues weighing me down is the Lord. I choose to posture myself toward Him instead of away from Him. One way to do this is to invite Him into the things I'm facing today.

## QUIET

This one can be especially hard when our minds are crowded and our feelings might be loud. Breath prayer can be a great way to quiet yourself. Breath in and breath out slowly while thinking of a few words or phrases from Scripture as your prayer.

## TRUST

Even if your feelings don't match, King David demonstrates throughout the Psalms that we can still choose to trust the Lord. We verbalize our decision to trust in the Lord even if that doesn't yet feel true.

---

## SHIFT IN FOCUS

Read today's verses once more, out loud if you can. Pause and respond to the Lord's invitation to engage with what is hard in your life with rest, returning, quiet, and trust.

Please borrow this prayer if it matches your heart:

Dear heavenly Father, thank You that I don't have to perform or prove anything to receive the rest You offer. I'll admit that it is hard to open my hands to what You're offering. I want to stay in control. I want to run away from what is hard in my life. It doesn't feel comfortable to name those things and hand them to You. But I don't want to be unwilling or unable to receive the help that will refresh and restore my very soul. Help my stubborn heart here. Help me to rest and allow You to fill me up. Help me to return to You, bringing You my problems. Help me be quiet. Help me to trust that Your heart is full of love toward me. Thank You for the way You love me, like a good parent does. Amen.

# DAY 48 • • • • • • • • • • • •

## The Temptation of Excess

*And do not get drunk with wine, for that is debauchery,*
*but be filled with the Spirit.*
(Ephesians 5:18)

*And he said to them, "Take care, and be on your guard*
*against all covetousness, for one's life does not consist in*
*the abundance of his possessions."*
(Luke 12:15)

When it comes to sloth, a little is never enough. A little nap, a little TV, a little treat. This is how we know that we are numbing instead of consciously choosing something that is helpful and restful to us. The loss of self-control around something good turns it into something harmful. One glass of wine turns into two bottles, for example.

The Bible has a lot to say about excess and gives us a couple of sobering examples of people who ultimately lost their relationship with God due to their desire for their own wealth, power, pleasure, or abundance—people like King Saul, King Solomon, Judas Iscariot, and Ananias and Sapphira.

We know that excess is not good for us, but when we are numbing on autopilot, we rarely stop to think about what is actually good for us.

In seasons of stress, these proclivities become all the more tempting to us. We need safeguards such as friends who will hold us accountable, consistent Bible time, and discipline.

A friend who is holding you accountable will need you to be honest about where you tend to struggle. Consistent Bible time will always be hard because the devil wants you to do *anything* other than reading your Bible and praying. Discipline might look like no TV during finals week, no drinking alcohol around the anniversary of your parent's death, or setting a timer to limit naps to seventeen minutes.

Only you can figure out what this looks like for you, but noticing your need for safeguards and setting them up gives you a fighting chance to not give into temptation.

---

## SHIFT IN FOCUS

Spend some time in prayer and ask God to reveal specific areas where you're tempted toward excess, especially in stress.

What's one safeguard you can put into place today that might help?

Once you decide, tell someone about this safeguard and ask them to keep you accountable.

# DAY 49 • • • • • • • • • • •

*Resting vs. Numbing*
*By Alison Bradley*

*Come to me, all who labor and are heavy laden, and I will give you*
*rest. Take my yoke upon you, and learn from me, for I am gentle*
*and lowly in heart, and you will find rest for your souls.*
*For my yoke is easy, and my burden is light.*
(Matthew 11:28–30)

**H**ow can you tell the difference between true rest and numbing?
I believe the Enneagram is beneficial to us because it reflects so
much more than our behaviors. The Enneagram helps us understand the motivation behind our behaviors.

Both rest and numbing have the potential to look identical
on the surface

You may take a nap to experience real rest…or you may take
a nap to avoid facing a wave of grief that is impacting you that
day.

You may read a good book to rest and enjoy a good story…
or you may read a good book to escape reality and not have to
engage in the work the Lord might be asking of you.

How can you tell the difference between the two? How are
you supposed to figure out when an activity is restful or numbing? A helpful way to determine the motivation behind your
behavior is to ask yourself, "Why?"

Why are you choosing this activity? Are you choosing this snack, this show, or this nap as a way to avoid something? Will this activity be refreshing? Will it help you to experience real peace and wholeness? Be as honest as you can with yourself. If you're not sure, invite the Lord to show you the condition of your heart and your true motivations here.

Another indicator to tell if you are resting or numbing is to determine how you feel on the other side of that activity. Do you feel rested and refreshed? Or do you feel grumpy, irritable, or just as empty as before? Do you feel a little more like yourself? Real rest doesn't mean we are *cured* or *fixed* from whatever is hard in our lives, but it does mean we put our hands out to receive real rest and provision from the Lord.

Read Psalm 23, which begins with the beautiful trusting statement, *"The LORD is my shepherd; I shall not want."* King David offers us powerful imagery of what real rest can look like. A meal in the presence of our enemies becomes a place where we get to experience the Lord's provision. Walking through *"the valley of the shadow of death"* (verse 4) becomes a place where we get to experience the Lord's comfort and presence. The circumstances are certainly not ideal in either of these images. But David's posture is one that is receptive to the Lord, looking for His presence in the midst of hard and difficult circumstances. You are invited to experience the same provision and peace as you let the Lord lead you and you feel His presence.

## SHIFT IN FOCUS

Pause to reread the words of Jesus in today's reading from the Gospel of Matthew, allowing yourself to imagine our Lord saying them to you. What tone is He using when He says these words?

Notice there is no shame if you labor and your task feels heavy. Jesus offers the compassionate invitation, *"Come to me."* He invites you to learn from Him. He is a gentle teacher who wants to help you find true rest for your soul.

Pause for a moment to respond to Jesus in prayer. What is stirring up in your heart as you hear this invitation from Him? Are you tired today? Are you feeling heavy and weary? How would you like to respond to what Jesus has said to you in these verses?

• • • • • • • • • • • • **DAY 50**

*Productive Rest*
*By Jena Stagner*

*Therefore do not be anxious about tomorrow, for tomorrow will be anxious for itself. Sufficient for the day is its own trouble.*
(Matthew 6:34)

God can do more with six of your days than you can do with seven. He is perfect and always accomplishes what He sets out to do. We see from the very beginning that God rested. This is the same rhythm of life to which He calls you.

As an Achiever, it is hard for you to disconnect from the consuming thoughts that come along with the open tasks. Responsibilities and commitments can fill up your schedule, leaving you with no opportunities to rest.

What we do with our rest is a direct reflection of what we believe. If you don't have enough time to do what you need to do in six days, you need to figure out why this is so.

Productive rest doesn't look like taking a day off and forgetting about all of your responsibilities. Instead, it's living six days with such intention that you have space to rest productively, trusting in God, who says your capacity requires rest.

You need sufficient rest as much as you need adequate sleep. When you live with one day of productive rest, you'll experience increased productivity during the other six days.

Beware of procrastinating your need for rest, believing that you have tomorrow so you don't need to worry about it today. Behind this lie is the unspoken belief that there isn't enough time or space for what you need to do. The procrastination then undermines the truth that productive rest is required to live the life God wants for you.

The rest God gives us is so productive that He calls us to work six days using the strength we've garnered from it. Current culture calls for us to work six days to get one day of rest. God calls us to the opposite: rest one day and receive the capacity to work for six.

When you are obedient to the Holy Spirit, there is a connection to working and resting God's way. Productive rest is founded in surrender and always leads to a better life.

## SHIFT IN FOCUS

Reflect on the past few weeks. Are you working seven days or intentional with only six? What could you do this week to be faithful to working six days and resting for one? Consider what you would need to do to model this rhythm of life. If you feel frustrated because you don't think you have enough time, consider how avoiding rest could be contributing to this.

If you're not ready to take a full day of rest, consider taking a few hours or half of a day and working up to twenty-four hours. Your rest day doesn't have to be on a Sunday. Consider what works for your schedule, and then figure out all the actions you'd need to take to make that happen.

If rest of any sort feels impossible, think about whether you're truly in a hectic season with an end in sight, or whether you're saying no to God and yes to something else. What is He calling you to do this week to live faithfully to the call of productive rest?

# 10 DAYS OF LOYALTY AND FEAR

*Going to Six in Growth*

## DAY 51 • • • • • • • • • • •

*Seasons of Growth*

*Every good gift and every perfect gift is from above,*
*coming down from the Father of lights, with whom there is no*
*variation or shadow due to change.*
(James 1:17)

**A**s we talked about in the beginning of our conversation about
stress, thinking of your life in seasonal terms is not only biblical,
but it also gives you a lot more grace and hope for your circumstances. Seasons of stress are the opposite of seasons of growth.
The latter are periods in your life in which you feel as if you have
room to breathe, have more energy, and can focus on spiritual,
mental, and physical growth.

Seasons of growth are often blurry or over-romanticized
when we look back at our life as a whole. We either can't remember

a time in our life that we didn't feel the hum of anxiety and stress, or we can't live fully in the present because no season will ever be as good as it has been in the past.

Both of these thought processes are unfruitful because they're extremes. There is always a mixture of good and bad in every situation; only the details change. This is a result of living in a fallen world. We are living outside of our natural habitat, and it often feels like a paradox of good and bad at the same time.

Now, this doesn't mean that seasons of stress and growth coexist all the time; often, they don't. Circumstances in our lives often tip the scales. Nothing is ever all bad or all good. Working in a toxic environment or the death of a loved one will send us into a season of stress. Likewise, getting our dream job, hitting a sweet spot with parenting, or flourishing in a good friendship can tip the scale to seasons of growth.

You should push yourself during seasons of growth. Have you been wanting to read a certain book or join a Bible study? Do it! Are you thinking about starting a diet or exercising more? Now's the time! We literally have more mental space, more energy, and more bandwidth when we are in seasons of growth.

We can also see a lot of encouraging behaviors pop up. Press into them and build them in a way that they'll stick beyond this season. Create good habits that will serve a future, stressed-out you. Consistent Bible reading is a must for all of life, but especially those hard days when you feel lost.

Growth seasons are the days of digging deep and reaping the rewards. These seasons are a gift from a heavenly Father who loves you and wants to give you good things.

As we see in 1 Peter 4:10, we should be using these seasons of *good gifts* to not only build up our faith, but also to help others. In the next nine days, you'll see how going to Six in growth helps you specifically with this.

---

## SHIFT IN FOCUS

Are you currently in a season of growth?

Do you have a couple of good seasons in your past that you might be over-romanticizing, or maybe are ungrateful for?

• • • • • • • • • • **DAY 52**

*The Best of Type Six*

> *A man of many companions may come to ruin,*
> *but there is a friend who sticks closer than a brother.*
> (Proverbs 18:24)

> *A friend loves at all times.*
> (Proverbs 17:17)

**B**efore we dive into a discussion of the best of type Six, often known as the Guardian, I need you to place whatever thoughts you have about Sixes to the side for a moment. Whether you know a Six personally or not, the stereotypes are loud and often negative in tone. If you, as a Three, don't have an accurate picture of Sixes, the practicality of your going to Six in growth can feel confusing.

Sixes are the most trustworthy, loyal, and diverse Enneagram type. They defend their beliefs, family, and ideals much more fiercely than they will defend themselves. They can be loud or quiet, meek or fiery, ambitious or satisfied with the status quo. All of these variables can make Sixes hard to type, but the two main threads that run throughout their lives are fear and loyalty.

A healthy Six might look nothing like the description of Sixes you have in your head. A truly healthy Six is an absolute sweetheart, carefully tending to the relationships and duties they have around them. They'll be fun, easygoing, courageous, and very relational, valuing loyalty over judgment in friendships. This makes them attractive to all Enneagram types. Their anxieties may continue to ebb and flow like waves, but chances are that only God will hear them spoken aloud.

Instead of clinging to authority for security, they'll come to fully grasp that humans will always fail and only God can give us the security we crave.

As a Three, you go to Six in growth through loyalty, fear, steadfastness, championing others instead of competing, and becoming a team player, just to name a few. Now, you might feel a bit defensive reading that list, as you may already have all or most of these qualities. And perhaps fear doesn't sound like something to grow in!

However, over the next eight days, we will unpack what going to Six in growth means and shine a light on some realities that you might not have noticed before.

---

## SHIFT IN FOCUS

Do you have any Sixes in your life?

What's something you admire about them?

In what ways are they strong where you are weak?

If you don't have an Enneagram Six in your life, I'd encourage you to listen to *Sleeping At Last*'s podcast episode on Sixes, or the song "Six" by the same composer. This podcast has transformed my view on type Sixes and given me so much more respect and grace for them.

• • • • • • • • • • • **DAY 53**

*How Do I Go to Six?*

*Let not steadfast love and faithfulness forsake you; bind them around your neck; write them on the tablet of your heart.*
(Proverbs 3:3)

The practicalities of going to Six in growth can feel hard to grasp when most of the information we hear about Sixes focuses on their anxiety and fear. But the strongest aspects of Sixes are areas where you, as a Three, may tend to be weak.

## LOYALTY

Loyalty is sticking with someone, something, or a belief system even if it's unpopular, the subject of mockery, or is simply just not impressive. In American culture, the closest examples we have of true loyalty usually have to do with sports teams. As a Three, you may tend to be more of a bandwagon fan of new and shiny things, ideas, or even people. Growing in loyalty means that your enthusiasm doesn't leave, even when something is no longer fresh or exciting.

## FEAR

Humility and fear go hand in hand for Threes. Usually, after an epic failure, you'll feel a more realistic fear about your own wisdom, abilities, and *rightness*. This type of fear is a necessity in the life of a healthy Three.

## BECOMING A TEAM PLAYER

As Achievers, Threes are naturally great leaders. With your initiative, energy, and forward thinking, it only makes sense for you to be leading the charge in most cases. However, we are all team members in some area or another. You can't lead *everything*, and as you grow, you won't feel the need to. When Threes lead, they tend to become distanced from the people they're leading. But like all of us, Threes need real relationships and community! Learning to be a team player like a Six instead of being the leader will really help you with this.

---

## SHIFT IN FOCUS

What aspect of an Enneagram Six do you feel like you need to grow in the most?

Which one have you really grown in?

If God is convicting you in one of these areas, try these tips to *"bind them around your neck; write them on the tablet of your heart"* (Proverbs 3:3):

+ Research what God says about growth in His Word.

+ Write out a Scripture quote on a sticky note that reminds you of your needed work in this area, and place it where you will see it often.

+ Ask for prayer from those in your community, being open about your need for growth in this area of your life.

• • • • • • • • • • • **DAY 54**

*Loyalty Over Competition*

> *Greater love has no one than this,*
> *that someone lay down his life for his friends.*
> (John 15:13)

**B**y its nature, a competition means that there will be a winner and a loser. It's only natural that in our life, we long to win; if we do, those we are competing against will lose by default.

During my childhood, my older brother was favored by people in our family, making me the perpetual loser in those relationships. As I tried to get the attention of these loved ones, my heart longed for my brother to feel the sting of being the loser. (It feels wrong to say that even now, but it's true.)

In humility, love, and kindness, there is no room for you to wish for someone else to lose so you can win. When you go to Six in growth, feeling a Guardian's special blend of loyalty and protection, you champion the people you love even if that means you may always be the loser.

Who in your life do you love? This might be family members, friends, or mentors. Perhaps you have a whole classroom of students, a church body, or a hurting group of people who are near and dear to your heart. No matter how short or long your list is, I want you to hold it in your mind for a moment. Feel the affection you have for these people in your heart, and let it permeate.

Loving these people means that you might lose, you might fail, and you might be wrong. That's okay. This is humility and loyalty; this is love in action.

When we are focused on loving others in the way that Christ loves us, winning or losing, and being first or last ceases to be important.

---

## SHIFT IN FOCUS

Are there people in your life whom you love, but you also struggle with being competitive against them?

Do you often compare yourself to them and feel shame or joy?

What would it look like for you to value love over competition in this relationship?

How can you let down your right to win here?

● ● ● ● ● ● ● ● ● ● ● ● **DAY 55**

*Choosing Faithfulness*
*By Jena Stagner*

> *See, I have set before you today life and good, death and evil.*
> *If you obey the commandments of the LORD your God that I*
> *command you today, by loving the LORD your God, by walking in*
> *his ways, and by keeping his commandments and his statutes and*
> *his rules, then you shall live and multiply, and the LORD your God*
> *will bless you in the land that you are entering to take possession of*
> *it. But if your heart turns away, and you will not hear,*
> *but are drawn away to worship other gods and serve them,*
> *I declare to you today, that you shall surely perish.*
> (Deuteronomy 30:15–18)

Looking at your day, you may not feel like you have much of a say in or even a choice about how it will go. Commitments and demands often drive us in a way that doesn't leave us feeling like we have options. Faith can then begin to feel like a burden and obligation—something you have to do to have the life you want. When you feel like you don't have a choice, the beauty of faith becomes stripped away.

When God created the world and everything in it, He made the Tree of Knowledge of Good and Evil. (See Genesis 2:9, 17.) With that tree, He created choice. Adam and Eve did not respond by choosing faithfulness. And after their incorrect decision and that original sin, God made a way to restore mankind to Himself despite their rebellion.

Later in Deuteronomy, we see God spell out this choice even more. He puts before us life and death, good and evil. Obedience to His Word and His ways always leads to life and goodness. And this choice is ever-present in every moment.

While it can feel overwhelming to live in a state in which you are always conscious of the choice between good and evil, this is a space where you are not alone. You have the ever-present connection with the Holy Spirit, who is always willing to lead the way.

What determines His leading is you acting or reacting to life. Choosing faithfulness comes from a connection to the present moment and seeing before you the choice of life and death, and in that space, choosing life.

The little choices may not feel like life or death at the moment, but each act of disobedience always leads to death, and each act of faithfulness always leads to life.

While this can lead to fear of taking the wrong action, God made a way so that no perfection is required here. If your perfection were possible, there would have been no need for Jesus to die on the cross. No matter how much we rebel against Him, God can work it together for good.

God has zero desire for you to choose death; He wants nothing more than for you to choose life by choosing to do what's right. But He knows your sin nature. He knows you may choose sin.

As we see in the garden, with Adam and Eve's sin, God provided the way for restoration. With each moment, you are choosing to act in faith or react in sin. And when you become aware of the latter, you can repent and begin again. Restoration is always made available on the other side of our repentance.

---

## SHIFT IN FOCUS

Do you feel like you've been in a state of reaction or action? If you've been reacting to life, what could you repent so that you can begin again, choosing life this time instead? Spend some time in prayer and ask what faithful steps God wants you to choose today.

If you feel like you are in a state of action and empowered by choice, what has helped you stay present to this? Are there any times in your week or day where you see disconnection happening and where choosing faithfulness is more challenging? How can you build on the momentum you have to continue choosing to act on your faithfulness throughout the days ahead?

# DAY 56 • • • • • • • • • •

*Healthy Fear*

*The fear of the LORD is hatred of evil.*
(Proverbs 8:13)

*Therefore, my beloved, as you have always obeyed, so now, not only as in my presence but much more in my absence, work out your own salvation with fear and trembling.*
(Philippians 2:12)

*But the LORD takes pleasure in those who fear him, in those who hope in his steadfast love.*
(Psalm 147:11)

The childhood story I've heard from many Threes goes something like this. "I was the oldest or filled the role of the oldest child in my family. I was aware at a young age of responsibilities, expectations, and how my appearance was perceived by others. I am close to my mom, or have always wished I were close to my mom; my dad was absent or overbearing. I was driven and socially likable in high school. It was important to me that teachers liked me."

Whether that fits your story precisely or not, there's one thing I've heard from almost every Three I've coached: "I grew up fast" This could be because of the realities of your family life, or just your own social awareness, but most Threes had a fair amount of responsibility by ages eight to ten.

Whatever happened in your life as a child, you didn't have the luxury of being scared, helpless, and dependent for very long. These are vital feelings for children to go through and process within the confines of a loving relationship with kind parents. But as we know, not every child has that. Children naturally get scared because their understanding is limited, and healthy processing of that fear looks like them running to a parent for comfort. However, many Threes didn't feel like they could do that with their parents, usually because of a perceived responsibility that they could not be childish or pose a burden.

Processing these feelings healthily as a child sets you up for having healthy feelings of self, safety, and trust as an adult. If you were unable to do so, you will struggle with the need to project an image instead of living in authenticity, having delusions of your own ability and lacking humility. You will struggle with being overly dependent or not trusting authority.

This is why going to Six in growth and being able to process fear is *vital* for Threes. It might feel like taking a step backward to process something you weren't able to in childhood. But facing fear and working through it will make you a stronger Achiever.

---

## SHIFT IN FOCUS

It can feel weird to talk about fear in a positive sense when the Bible says "*fear not*" so often. However, healthy fear—such as fearing God, fearing danger, and having realistic expectations—helps us grow closer to the Lord. In the Scripture readings for today, God tells us to work out our faith with fear and trembling.

Set aside time where you can be still and quiet. In a journal or notebook, write down some fears you had as a child, then state who you should've felt safe to go to with those fears. Grieve the fact that you didn't feel like you could be comforted then, and let God comfort you now.

This *will* feel uncomfortable, but that's how you know you're exercising a part of you that is out of shape. Over time, you'll probably start to remember instances that you need to grieve with God, and His comfort will start to feel more palpable.

• • • • • • • • • • • **DAY 57**

*Humility in Leadership*
*By Jena Stagner*

*Therefore, we are ambassadors for Christ,*
*God making his appeal through us.*
*We implore you on behalf of Christ, be reconciled to God.*
(2 Corinthians 5:20)

*With all humility and gentleness, with patience,*
*bearing with one another in love.*
(Ephesians 4:2)

**W**ith your ambition as a Three comes a desire to lead…and along with this desire is our fallen nature and propensity toward sin. As a result, it can be tempting to either lead with pride or fall to the other side and believe that you are incapable of being a leader.

The call of your holy ambition is for the good of others and for God's glory to be known. To be effective at this requires humility and leadership. There is no space for making it about you or hiding from what God is calling you to do.

Humility takes action from a place of surrender and trust, faithfully walking out each step of obedience.

Jesus gave us a model to follow, and Luke 22:42 speaks directly to it:

*"Father, if you are willing, remove this cup from me. Nevertheless, not my will, but yours, be done."*

Your flesh will want to take the easy road, and your sinful nature will desire that you choose your flesh in pride over humility to God's will. This is the ever-present battle of a leader.

God calls you to be an ambassador, which is a leadership position. You living as an ambassador of Christ is the model God created as the most effective way to make His message known.

Your role in this requires humility and action in alignment with your leadership. God wants you to make a difference in this world by spreading His love and His Word.

This leadership style is upside down from the hustle and drive we see in our society, which doesn't see humility, gentleness, or patience as useful in leadership.

But as Christians, we are called to lead with humility and bear with one another. There is no climbing a ladder or getting to the top by pushing others down. There is only the ground-floor work of making a difference in the lives of everyone you know and meet.

While it may be hard to believe that leaders with humility can change the world, God clearly says this is the case. (See, for example, Proverbs 29:23; Matthew 11:29; 1 Peter 5:5.) There is no need to move to the other side of the country for it to happen. When we live out humility in our leadership, we are bringing Christ's light to others.

God so loved the world that He sent His only Son. This is God's will, and He desires it to be made known. When you act with humility, you don't shrink away from your responsibilities but act with confidence. Bearing with one another may not feel like leadership, but this is the work of your Savior.

Your leadership with ambition for God's will is needed out in the world, and your humility will keep you effective in this.

## SHIFT IN FOCUS

Do you believe you're a leader?

How could you own your leadership role as an ambassador for Christ?

Into which areas of your life could you bring humility, gentleness, patience, and bearing another's burdens?

In prayer, create a vision for what leadership with humility might look like in your life.

If there are any areas you're struggling with, write them out and surrender them to Jesus. Spend time in prayer, share with God what you want for these areas, and ask Him to lead the way.

# DAY 58 • • • • • • • • • •

*The Issue with Loyalty*

*A faithful man will abound with blessings, but whoever hastens to be rich will not go unpunished.*
(Proverbs 28:20)

The concept of disloyalty can feel very disconcerting. We all tend to think we are loyal and loving—at least when situations warrant our loyalty. However, loyalty is something that you, as a Three, tend to struggle with in one way or another.

You may be very loyal to your family, work, or even your local coffee shop, but Threes tend to struggle with being loyal to anything that's not a foundation in their life.

Your new friend starts to feel a bit clingy, so you disappear. Your pastor doesn't seem to value you, so you leave the church. You start a project, announcing your ideas and vision to those around you, but don't follow through on your big plans. You may never realize the impact you have or how many people count on you. Being future-focused means you're often on to the next thing before finishing something else or formally acknowledging that you're done with a current project.

This can hurt other people and leave them in a lurch. For this reason, they may view you as a disloyal person. I know it stings to hear this, but it is likely very true.

This is why a loyal and growing Three doesn't make commitments or promises without following through. They're honest with themselves and others before ending a relationship, plan, or organization. They're up-front and communicate when they're losing steam or don't think a relationship will work out.

Avoiding an issue, or moving on without discussion, is seen by many other Enneagram types as abandonment.

---

## SHIFT IN FOCUS

Are you often in haste? Today's verse from Proverbs talks about faithfulness and haste in some very stern terms. Faithfulness can mean you'll need to be patient and stick with something when you'd rather not. It might mean that you risk losing something that "could be better." But being faithful to your commitments is a blessing to those who are depending on you.

Have you been convicted about an area of your life where you have not been loyal?

What would it look like to communicate to that person, team, or organization now?

# DAY 59 • • • • • • • • • • • •

*The Listening Three*
*By Jena Stagner*

*Know this, my beloved brothers: let every person be quick to hear,*
*slow to speak, slow to anger.*
(James 1:19)

*Do nothing from selfish ambition or conceit,*
*but in humility count others more significant than yourselves.*
(Philippians 2:3)

As someone driven to achieve, you may be tempted to live in light of your own agenda. As a result, it's easy to see people as an interruption and not what matters most.

When you count others as more significant than your agenda, however, you can give up listening to your selfish ambition—your thoughts, feelings, and considerations. When you give that up, you can connect with God's ambition, which is loving the world and making His love known.

A powerful way to make His love known is to be *someone who listens.*

In growth, this ability to listen and connect is available for you in a powerful way. When you leave space for other people, counting them more significant than yourself, you empower them and your relationship grows stronger.

And when you genuinely connect with others from a place of vulnerability rather than a place of concern for looking good or getting it right, a true connection can begin to happen where you can share your light.

Here are a few steps you can take to develop your listening skills:

+ Prioritize listening to God first. Finding time to be still, pray, read your Bible, and wait on the Lord at the beginning of your day will bring you closer to Him and others in your life.

+ Seek to stay connected and open to the Holy Spirit to gain a supernatural connection with God's will. This will help you navigate how to listen powerfully to others.

+ Stay focused on what people are saying and disconnect from the noise in your head that wants to change them, fix them, or give them the right answer. They don't need you to prove your adequacy. They simply need a space to share their needs and concerns. When you have an agenda playing in your head as you listen, this is evidence you aren't actually hearing them.

+ Listen for the good. Some people feel the need to vent their frustrations to others. If someone trusts you with this, give them space, but don't connect with it. Don't agree, disagree, or put in your two cents. Just let them speak. When you hear something positive, focus on that. Hear what they are saying and provide affirmation that goodness still exists in this world.

Listening is a skill you can develop over time by being mindful and thoughtful about other people's feelings and expectations. Continue to press and grow into this space. Be curious, listen from a place of love, and do all you can to point them to Christ by sharing in vulnerability.

When you listen effectively, it gives you the ability to connect with others and have space to share how Christ has made the difference in your life.

---

## SHIFT IN FOCUS

How well do you think you listen?

Do you see others as an interruption to your day?

Who in your life will you talk with utilizing this new level of listening? Pick one of the actions from above and work to live that out. If your day doesn't give space for conversations, set up a time with someone in your life to talk with them and truly listen. As you listen, find areas to connect and vulnerably share how God is working in your life in that area.

● ● ● ● ● ● ● ● ● ● ● **DAY 60**

*The Honest Three*

*Practice these things, immerse yourself in them,*
*so that all may see your progress.*
(1 Timothy 4:15)

$\mathbf{A}$t first, prioritizing growth may not feel like accomplishing much; in fact, it may feel like giving up. Every moment you are convicted to remain loyal, or dive into fear and don't, the reality of growth moves further away from the reality in your head. Again and again, you may fail to take action on prioritizing these things because it just feels too hard or the results don't come quickly enough…and then you may feel beaten down and hopeless for change.

This is the challenge of being motivated by worth. It is the challenge of wanting to grow but being afraid that if you don't come across as valuable to those around you, you won't be. Or maybe you believe that you can't change. These feelings are something Satan uses to make sure you never walk in the freedom of your worth in Christ.

Satan is all about stopping your growth from coming to fruition. I wouldn't be surprised if you even notice elements of spiritual attack as you prioritize growth, but that doesn't mean growth isn't God's heart for you.

Going to Six in growth will feel painful at times, and you'll get discouraged. Remember that life is seasonal and you will not achieve your *ultimate* state of growth here on earth. You cannot become your ideal self in this life because you will never be without a sin nature while you're still breathing. However, this doesn't mean that you are not growing. By the power of the Holy Spirit, you are in the process of a beautiful becoming.

Don't let two steps forward and one step back discourage you. This is still moving forward; this is still growing.

Fear, humility, and loyalty may feel out of reach or not big enough to actually change your heart, but you can trust God for the outcome. You can trust that love is better than the satisfaction of winning. You're trusting God's Word, for He said He is *"the God of hope"* (Romans 15:13), and that hope is something He wants for you. Like a child at the edge of a swimming pool jumping into their father's arms, you're trusting that God is ready to catch you.

---

## SHIFT IN FOCUS

Here, we are going to use 1 Timothy 4:15 as a guideline for action:

> *Practice these things, immerse yourself in them, so that all may see your progress.*

## "PRACTICE THESE THINGS"

Every new thing you've ever done required practice. Growing by going to Six is no different. Practice by communicating when you feel like you're losing steam and being honest about it. Plan time to dive into childhood fear, choose one action that can be your next right thing, and tell the devil to take a hike when he tries to make you feel shame. You are precious in God's sight and He is proud when you take steps to follow Him.

## "IMMERSE YOURSELF IN THEM"

What verse that we mentioned over the last ten days really stuck out to you? I would encourage you to memorize it, write it out, and post it someplace where you will see it every day. Immerse yourself in the truth of your worth in Christ, and you'll find yourself slowly but surely believing it to be true.

## "SO THAT ALL MAY SEE YOUR PROGRESS."

Pick a couple of people in your life with whom you can share your big or small victories. I hope you have a couple of people who come to mind right away, but if you don't, there are plenty of Instagram or Facebook pages for Threes with followers who would love to cheer you on in your Three-ish wins. Be bold and share them as something worth celebrating. Go get yourself a coffee or an ice cream cone! Life is hard, and any victories are worth celebrating with God and others.

# BOOK RECOMMENDATIONS FOR THREES

Steve Wiens, *Whole: Restoring What Is Broken in Me, You, and The Entire World* (Colorado Springs, CO: NavPress, 2017)

Donald Miller, *Scary Close: Dropping the Act and Finding True Intimacy* (Nashville, TN: Nelson Books, 2014)

Tish Harrison Warren, *Liturgy of the Ordinary: Sacred Practices in Everyday Life* (Downers Grove, IL: InterVarsity Press, 2016)

Leeana Tankersley, *Breathing Room: Letting Go So You Can Fully Live* (Grand Rapids, MI: Revell, 2014)

Paul Vischer, *Sidney and Norman: A Tale of Two Pigs* (Nashville, TN: Tommy Nelson, 2006)

Timothy Keller, *Every Good Endeavor: Connecting Your Work to God's Work* (New York, NY: Penguin Books, 2014)

Gem and Alan Fadling, *What Does Your Soul Love? Eight Questions That Reveal God's Work in You* (Downers Grove, IL: IVP Books, 2019)

Henry Cloud and John Townsend, *Boundaries: When to Say Yes, How to Say No to Take Control of Your Life* (Grand Rapids, MI: Zondervan, 1992)

Robert D. Jones, *Pursuing Peace: A Christian Guide to Handling Our Conflicts* (Wheaton, IL: Crossway, 2012)

As the Enneagram has passed through many hands, and been taught by various wonderful people, I want to acknowledge that none of the concepts or ideas of the Enneagram have been created by me. I'd like to give thanks to the Enneagram teachers and pioneers who have gone before me, and whose work has influenced this devotional:

Suzanne Stabile

Ian Morgan Cron

Father Richard Rohr

Don Richard Riso

Russ Hudson

Beatrice Chestnut

Beth McCord

Ginger Lapid-Bogda

# ABOUT THE AUTHOR

Elisabeth Bennett first discovered the Enneagram in the summer of 2017 and immediately realized how life-changing this tool could be. She set out to absorb all she could about this ancient personality typology, including a twelve-week Enneagram Certification course taught by Beth McCord, who has studied the Enneagram for more than twenty-five years.

Elisabeth quickly started her own Enneagram Instagram account (@Enneagram.Life), which has grown to more than 70,000 followers. Since becoming a certified Enneagram coach, Elisabeth has conducted more than three hundred one-on-one coaching sessions, focused on helping her clients find their type and apply the Enneagram to their lives for personal and spiritual growth. She has also conducted staff/team building sessions for businesses and high school students.

Elisabeth has lived in beautiful Washington State her entire life and now has the joy of raising her own children there with her husband, Peter.

To contact Elisabeth, please visit:

www.elisabethbennettenneagram.com

www.instagram.com/enneagram.life